Win
the
Happiness
Game

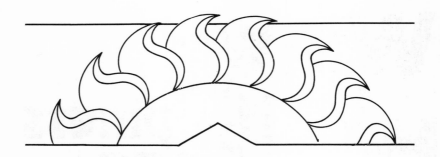

"I am impressed by *Win the Happiness Game*, the unique and practical book by Dr. William Nickels. It offers sound and workable suggestions for finding real fulfillment in life. Since it made me happy just to read the book, one would surely develop deeper joy following Dr. Nickel's wise thoughts.**"**

Dr. Norman Vincent Peale

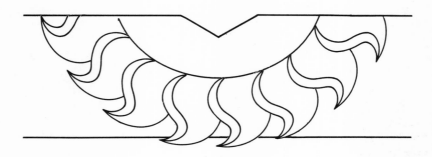

Win the Happiness Game

Dr. William Nickels

Foreword by
Dr. Warren Johnson

A ACROPOLIS BOOKS LTD.

ACROPOLIS BOOKS LTD.
Colortone Building, 2400 17th St.,
N.W., Washington, D.C. 20009

158.1

NIC

Printed in the United States of America by
COLORTONE PRESS Creative Graphics, Inc.
Washington, D.C. 20009

Library of Congress Cataloging in Publication Data

Nickels, William G
   The happiness game.

   Includes index.
   1. Happiness. 2. Success. I. Title.
BF575.H27N52   158'.1   80-29884
ISBN 0-87491-070-6   AACR1

Dedication

To my parents who showed me how to live a joyful life; to my friends who support me on my journey; and to Marsha and Joel who give me unconditional love.

Acknowledgements

My father's lifelong example of living fully and joyfully each day inspired me to write this book. If it were a particularly nice day, my Dad would take the day off from work (he was a salesman) and take my Mom and brothers and sisters for a drive through the country. Dad knew the importance of a balanced life and, by his example, became a model for everyone he met, especially me.

I learned a great deal from my friends as well. By sharing with me their joy as well as their pain, these friends became an inspiration. Many of them had to suffer through painful divorces, unrewarding jobs, and the like before they redirected their lives toward more joyful living. Special thanks go to John Engle for encouraging me to write this book and for showing me that one has to take risks to find new pleasures in life.

Gary Ford, Fred and Hillary Schneider, and Ron Gorman led me into personal growth seminars where I discovered new concepts. Countless numbers of my friends gave their time to read the manuscript and share their experiences with me. I thank them all.

Finally, I want to thank Sandy Friedman Alpert and all the staff at Acropolis Books for their help and encouragement.

No one can research a book about happiness without realizing the importance of God to a full and meaningful life. I want to thank God for His understanding and His gift of love for me. Without His guidance, I could not share my love with you.

Contents

THE HAPPINESS GAME

Contents

viii

Foreword

I am enthusiastic about Dr. William Nickels' new book, *Win the Happiness Game,* for a number of reasons. In the first place, I think it a healthy sign that people are increasingly able to come forward with the statement that they attach top priority in life to happiness. This is in the face of a long tradition which has held that happiness, fun and pleasure are basically unworthy conditions sought by the less firm of character. In the past, happiness has been viewed as more properly an occasional and brief bi-product of or respite from holding the nose to the grindstone. Dr. Nickels makes no bones about his ranking of happiness at the head of the pecking order of human values, making it

THE HAPPINESS GAME

clear that without happiness, other values are empty. Success is being happy!

One of the key messages of this book proves that Bobbie Burns was wrong: happiness *does* come when sought — if you know how to seek it and are willing to work at it. In other words happiness is not a will o' the wisp, evasive something out there. Rather it is a skill which can be taught and learned and used daily for the enrichment of life throughout life. How remiss we educators are that children are not taught this most valuable of life skills!

I am, perhaps, especially concerned about the whole subject and appreciative of Dr. Nickels' contribution because of two of the major adventures of my own life. The first of these is the clinic program* for children with various kinds of mental and physical disabilities that I have conducted for the past quarter of a century. In this program, we train volunteer college students (about seventy-five per semester) to work in a special way in a fun environment (gym, play rooms, etc.) with the children one on one. A major and rather unique feature of our training curriculum is that it emphasizes techniques of "goofusing" — our word for being silly, clowning around, having fun — sometimes in the most slapstick kinds of ways.

One of the common characteristics of the children referred to our program is that they have not had much fun in life and have known little happiness. Warm friendliness plus getting drawn into an absurd "Keystone Cops" episode or "silly walk" contest or whatever, may be the child's first step into the realm of relaxing and just having fun. Our program is very seriously therapeutic in intent, so of course fun-activitiy progresses in terms of the children's needs. But the basic ingredient in our therapy remains fun — which makes the children very active participants in their own therapy. (Mothers complain that clinic morning is the only one when they can get their kids up, and it's

*Children's Health & Developmental Clinic, University of Maryland, College Park, Maryland.

always hard to get them to leave when their hour is up.) Thousands of children have evidently benefited from our friendly-fun approach, and carefully controlled research has tended to verify many of the testimonials from parents and referring specialists in schools and medical programs.

In other words, our long experience demonstrates the validity of some of Dr. Nickels' major contentions — namely that happiness is a skill that can be learned, and that the practice of happiness is what I call "growthful," regardless of the individual's condition. Happiness encourages personality growth in Maslow's sense of self-actualization. Life is enriched by it regardless of whether the child is merely clumsy, socially inept or even dying. Adults have the same right to self actualization through happiness.

A second major adventure in my own life that makes me hope that Dr. Nickels' book will be widely used — not just read — is my own long bout with a rare but deadly disease. I have told the story of the first years of my battle with scleroderma in the book *So Desperate the Fight: An Innovative Approach to Chronic Illness*. Those were very tough years, and they have become still tougher recently as the disease has moved relentlessly into my internal vital organs: heart, lungs, kidneys and liver. But somewhere in the book I comment: "Still, these have been some of the best years of my life." How can this be so? How could anyone consider them "good years" when a mysterious disease seems systematically and implacably to be devastating a person's body?

Fortunately for me, I learned at an early age to follow Epictitus' admonition that a wise person could live happily in a trash heap. When I was a child I was in a situation that seemed quite miserable until it occured to me that it did not have to be miserable if only I would perceive it otherwise. So I looked about for little ways in which I could enjoy myself in spite of everything — and lo! I was soon quite happily engaged in various things. What a lesson!

THE HAPPINESS GAME

Noting that there were two basic steps in my "trick", (1) controlling my own perception of situations, and (2) taking action in the pursuit of interests (enjoyment), I began living a lot of my life in terms of that trick. Of course I sometimes forgot to use it and found myself at the mercy of events; but generally speaking, I tried creating happiness for myself. (Indeed I found that writings in the stoic tradition were full of suggestions about what Bertrand Russell was to call the "pursuit of happiness.") So various periods in my life which might be described as grim — some associated with academics, some with domestic problems and still others with having been a Marine Corps fighter pilot in World War II — were for the most part periods of enjoyment more than they were of grimness.

Thus, when the disease struck when I was about fifty — nearly ten years ago — I did not have to start from scratch in knowing how to make life worthwhile in spite of life-destroying obstacles. That is why I am honestly able to say that these have been some of the good years of my life. Much practice over the years has prepared me well for playing the happiness game, even in less than ideal circumstances.

Of course, my enthusiasm for *Win the Happiness Game,* and certain other of the self-help books, is based on what they have to offer in the way of helping people to improve the quality of their lives regardless of what life might bring. *By demystifying happiness and "reducing" it to a skill that can be learned through practice like any other skill, Dr. Nickels helps make it available to those who do not care to spend their lives groping about in the wrong places — in possessions, conquests, or such like — for the essence of what makes life worthwhile.* My own book focuses upon application of these basic ideas when adversity strikes but the individual decides to live on.

What better preparation for now and for whatever the future may hold than well developed and tested skills in the "happiness game?"

Warren R. Johnson

Introduction

*T*his book is my handbook to happiness. It is set up as a game because I find it fun to approach life as a contest. The goal is to bring into life self-awareness, self-satisfaction, generosity, and happiness. I wanted to share the game with others, so I established certain rules, ways of practicing, and procedures for selecting partners. I wanted to measure my progress, so I set up a scoring system. I call this book *Win the Happiness Game* because it is truly a plan for achieving happiness. Happiness is a skill that can be learned. I define happiness as the *ability* to appreciate fully who we are, what we have, and life the way it is now. Each of us holds the key to our own happiness.

THE HAPPINESS GAME

When we were teenagers, my friends and I were happy with what we had. We had friends, we had time for fun, and we had enough money to do what we wanted. Life was really great then.

We all made plans for the future. Fred planned to be a doctor.* Jim planned to make enough money to travel the world. Jack and I planned to go to college. We just knew we'd make it big one day. My friends and I were not the stars in high school — we didn't play football, we weren't in the senior play, and we didn't win any scholarships. We were average-achievers, but we were determined. We knew that all it took to be a success in this country was a great deal of hard work and a little bit of luck. Someday we would be rich, and *then* we would be happy! That was our inspiration.

The years flew by, and we all reached our goals. Fred was a successful surgeon with a wife and three children. Jim inherited some money and retired to a country estate. Jack was a professional salesman with a good income and the things money can bring. How exciting — life was working just as we planned.

We did regret that our search for success had taken us to separate cities though. We missed the joy of being with old friends. So one winter, my wife Marsha and I visited some of our old friends. Our first visit was to see Fred and his family. When we arrived, there was much celebrating and discussion about how well we were doing. Fred showed us his lovely home and spacious yard, his fancy sports car, his motorcycle, and his suite of offices at the hospital. We were delighted to share these successes with him.

But in the midst of all this joy, there seemed to be something missing. Fred seemed proud of all he had accomplished, but he didn't seem content. In fact, Fred told me something that changed my whole outlook on life. He said he wasn't very happy. In his struggle to become a doctor, he had been forced to give up many things. He did not

Names in this book have been changed to protect the privacy of individuals.

cultivate many friends, he did not spend much time with his family, and his life simply wasn't working the way he wanted.

Fred used an analogy to describe what he thought happened. He was like an octopus with many tentacles. The tentacles were called friends, family, fun, free time, recreation, and medicine. To be successful at medicine, Fred had to sacrifice the other tentacles for a while. He concentrated his efforts on the most important tentacle — medicine. His strategy worked. He became a successful doctor. But when he was ready to switch his attention to the other tentacles, after years of neglect, they had atrophied. When he tried to use the tentacles of friends and family, they simply weren't functioning. Fred knew that the struggle to regain those life-giving tentacles would be difficult, but he was eager to try. He was successful; now he wanted to be happy.

I had always believed that success was the bridge to happiness. Once you crossed that bridge and had money, fame, ... and everything else that goes with success, happiness was a natural consequence. But Fred showed me that for him success was *not* the bridge to happiness.

Later, Marsha and I visited Jack. Jack really had it made. He was young, single, president of a ski club, and launched on a great career path. Again, Marsha and I were thrilled to share the success of a close friend. But Jack also shared some misgivings about life. He did not feel comfortable at his job because he was being pressured to sell equipment his customers didn't need. And he really wasn't doing what he enjoyed. He thought he could be happier in the restaurant business because he loved to cook and enjoyed pleasing other people. Like Fred, Jack was successful but still searching for happiness.

We learned from Fred and Jack that our friend Jim was having problems. He had gone through a divorce and was living in relative prosperity. But he wasn't showing his customary enthusiasm and love of life.

THE HAPPINESS GAME

xv

When Marsha and I returned home, we were shaken. Life seemed to be going so well for all of our friends, but they really did not seem happy. We began discussing these experiences with our friends in Maryland, and the same trends emerged. We talked to many successful people, and although their circumstances were different, their *feelings* were similar: they were successful but they weren't happy.

We had heard of the mid-life crisis but this was the first time we realized what it meant in people's lives. We saw some of our college friends get divorced and suffer terrible trauma. We saw some friends abandon their successful careers and move "closer to nature." We saw some people so confused that they didn't know where to turn for help.

Shortly after Marsha and I became aware of these struggles, the book and magazine market became flooded with similar stories. We were particularly interested in books like *PASSAGES* and *TRANSFORMATIONS* that documented case after case of mid-life crisis, marriage trauma, career distress, retirement blues, and more. The experiences of our friends and these books led us to explore our own lives and to seek ways of avoiding unhappiness.

I had been reading books about transcendental meditation (TM), transactional analysis (TA), Zen, and the like. My Ph.D. is in the behavioral sciences, so I am familiar with the literature from psychology, sociology, social-psychology, and the other behavioral disciplines. But my experiences with my friends led me back to the literature to learn as much as possible about strategies for becoming successful *and* being happy along the way. I read hundreds of books and found some basic principles that I put to use in my own life. I began sharing these ideas and learned from my sharing how others managed the ups and downs of everyday living.

One colleague told me about his experiences in going through a divorce. He was miserable and some neighbors recommended he take a course called est (Erhard Seminars Training). After the first weekend session, he was thrilled. He had cleared up some problems with his parents and felt great about himself. He said he had gotten his money's worth already and still had another weekend to go. I was skeptical! After the second weekend, he was even more enthusiastic and urged me to go. After much prodding, I reluctantly agreed.

The training exceeded my expectations and was a positive experience. One thing I learned was the *happiness is a skill that can be learned.* I actually saw 250 people become more loving, more self-assured, and happier. I shared my excitement with others, including my wife, and encouraged her to go. She decided to explore Lifespring, a similar kind of training program. Marsha loved Lifespring and persuaded me to go too. I never had a more interesting and more loving long weekend. I learned to open up more, to be more honest, and to be more loving toward others. I felt really good about myself. Later, I took a course called Insight which created similar results.

Some people are hesitant to take courses such as est and Lifespring. Recently an ABC television report on 20/20 frightened people away from Lifespring by associating it with unpopular cults and by pointing out potential risks. This book gives people an opportunity to learn the concepts from personal development courses without personally attending them. The exercises in this book can be performed in the safe, protective environment of one's own home, surrounded by friends and family. I personally found Lifespring and other personal development courses very safe and protective. Nonetheless, I found it difficult to get others to attend. So I began discussing the concepts, and I have incorporated the best of these along with my own strategies in this book.

When people heard about my research into happiness and self-development, they asked me to talk about it in Sunday School and at club meetings. I found people very receptive to the concepts and noticed that they sometimes changed their lives dramatically by applying a few simple principles.

One friend always got upset when he was tied up in traffic. We discussed some techniques for handling his anger, and his life is now much better because he starts and ends his day relaxed rather than tense.

The wife of one of my dearest friends died of cancer. His sense of grief was overwhelming. But using the happiness principles, he experienced the pain of loss and moved forward to explore new beginnings.

My wife's friend and her husband lost the family savings in a business venture. The sense of failure was almost too much to bear. The temptation was to give up, but personal development concepts showed this family that life is a process and that to fail does not mean that people are failures. Experiencing the loss led to a determination to try again which resulted in a feeling of control that far exceeded anything they had ever experienced before.

Sharing these experiences taught me that life is full of ups and downs and that such experiences enhance people's ability to handle future set-backs and to appreciate joyful times as they come. But beyond that, I learned that people can learn to create more joy in their lives and to minimize despair. I found techniques for dealing with anger, fear, worry, and other negative emotions. Together my friends and I practiced these new-found skills.

I took copious notes throughout this period of self discovery. I enjoyed reviewing my notes periodically and rediscovering concepts that I had forgotten. Eventually, life became a game for me — a game in which I practiced sharing with others and being more joyful, more relaxed, and more loving. It was my own personal happiness game. I actually kept score at the end of the day (mentally at first), noting whether I was kind to others, how well I managed stress, and so on. It was great fun looking at my life as a semi-detached observer. I noticed what made me nervous, what made me angry, and what made me happy. These observations formed the foundation for a game strategy that improved my life.

I shared my game concepts with my wife, my neighbors, my students, and others. They, too, began playing, and we had fun sharing our successes and failures. But we often forgot some basic principles as we reverted to our lifelong patterns of behavior. Some of my acquaintances became frustrated because they kept reverting to former habits. But, by forming discussion groups, we supported one another and encouraged each other to keep trying. The little day-to-day victories over anger or worry became causes for celebration and incentives to go even further.

I personally wanted some way to keep track of my life. I wanted to set some meaningful goals and follow my progress. I wanted to find peace of mind and happiness. I wanted to be more loving to others, and I wanted to contribute to my community.

It's almost time to introduce the game itself, but first, I want you to make an agreement with yourself and me. If you're ready, I want you to *commit* yourself to this quest for happiness by signing a contract. If you're not yet ready, that's fine. Once you read through the book, then I'm sure you'll be ready to pledge yourself to the "no lose" goal of happiness.

At the end of the book, I will discuss personal development courses that could support you in your search for self-fulfillment. This book is the most comprehensive coverage of self-help concepts ever written. It will serve as your manual as you pursue selected topics in more depth. It will also serve as a personal score card that will show you your progress in the happiness game. Let's begin the game by covering some of the basic rules and concepts.

THE HAPPINESS CONTRACT

I want to experience success, joy, and contentment. I am committed 100% to reaching these goals and I am willing to practice the skills I need to accomplish them.

I will notice when my attitudes, thoughts, beliefs, and feelings get in my way of experiencing joy now. I want to be happy now and to be all I can be.

I am ready to play the happiness game.

Signature _____

Date _____

RULES OF THE GAME

1. Nobody is obligated to play the happiness game. There are people who go through life being bitter, sarcastic, and mean. That is their right. The temptation is to try to convince such people to change their ways and find the joy that life can bring. But that is against the rules. Everyone has the right to play the game *or not* play the game. Learn to play the game yourself. If you wish, show others how your life has improved and attract them to the game by example.

2. You cannot quit in the middle of the game. There is no particular time period within which the game must be played. Nonetheless, you must commit yourself to finishing one complete game. You can always quit for a while and practice a needed skill, but there should be a commitment at the beginning to stick it out at least once. And there are no excuses for quitting. Sickness, deaths in the family, business trips, and so on are not reasons for dropping out of the game. In fact, such occurences should get you to play with more determination. When happiness seems to be unreachable, that is the time the happiness game is most beneficial.

THE HAPPINESS GAME

3. You keep your own score. The only competition is between your score now and your score later. There are no bad scores, and no good scores, only scores that reveal progress. There is no perfect score; nobody feels happy all the time. There are no good players or bad players, just players who have reached different levels of happiness. All players have room for improvement.

4. Do not cheat. If you falsify your scores, you only cheat yourself. You must be totally honest with yourself. Don't be critical, just notice where you are in each category and record the score. Remember, there are no good or bad scores, only scores that reveal your progress in attaining your goals.

5. You must set your own goals. No one else can tell you what you must work on to be all you want to be. Each person has a specific goal. Ultimately, the basic goal—to experience happiness—is the same, but at any given time, each player will be working on a different element of the game.

There are no other *written* rules. There are unwritten rules that you'll learn as you play. For example, you should never deliberately hurt others in your attempt to reach your goals. You should not brag to others about how successful you are at some skills. You can share your joy at getting better, but never make others feel bad about their own progress if it is slower. You get the idea. Other rules will become clear as you play.

Chapter 1

Principles of the Game

*P*eople who say "I'm a success, why aren't I happy?" have learned that winning the games we play does not always bring happiness. To feel happy, we have to *experience* success. That is, we have to *feel* like winners, we have to *feel* content, and we have to *feel* successful.

The object of *The Happiness Game* is to experience happiness. Happiness to most people means having the experience of joy, pleasure, and contentment. When we are happy, we are pleased with ourselves, glad to be alive, and experience a general feeling of well-being. We feel lucky, successful, and fortunate. In short, happy people like things the way they are.

DEFINING THE TERMS

The purpose of this first chapter is to introduce you to the happiness game and how it is played. Let's begin by defining some terms we will be using:

> *Happiness* is the ability to appreciate fully who we are, what we have, and life the way it is now.
>
> A *game* is any test of mental or physical skill.
>
> An *ability* is something you have or can develop that gives you the skill to do something.
>
> To *experience happiness* means to be joyous, self-satisfied, and content.

Given these terms, we can talk about the happiness game. It is one of the best games I have ever played. It can be played by anyone, it can be played anywhere, and it is always challenging.

I would like you to enjoy the happiness game as much as I have. But at first you may feel uncomfortable with some of the procedures. When I learned to play golf, I felt very uncomfortable with the grip I was taught. The same was true of tennis. Many of the movements felt awkward and I couldn't believe that I would ever feel at ease with such different ways of playing. You may feel similar discomfort with the happiness game. Some of the principles may seem naive. Others will conflict with your beliefs. But that is true of almost all games at first. Nevertheless, if you practice, the behavior will become almost automatic. Give it a try; you can't win if you don't play.

The principles in *Win The Happiness Game* are not new. They have been formulated since the beginning of mankind and have been recorded in books as diverse as the Bible, sales manuals, and psychology texts. They are the accumulated wisdom of people such as Montaigne, Cicero, Emerson, and James. Even though they were developed years ago, many of the ideas are very relevant today. And that's why this book is important. In *Win the Happiness Game,* I have presented the concepts that worked the best for my friends and myself. Using our successes and failures as guides, I have pulled together all the principles that helped us become happy. Surely they will help you become happy too. And you'll be spared the trials and errors we suffered along the way to happiness.

OBJECTIVES OF THE GAME

The first objective of the game is to appreciate fully *who you are.* You are a perfect you, and yet it is unlikely that you feel perfect. Let's see if we can't put this in some perspective. Think of a flower. A flower is perfect even when it is a seed. Contained within that seed are all the ingredients for a perfect flower. A flower is also perfect when it is a bud. There is still much growing to take place, but there is nothing "wrong" with a flower at that stage; it is perfect. Eventually a flower will blossom and reveal all its inner beauty. Again, it is perfect. Eventually the flower will fade and die, but it will *still* be perfect. *It is whole and complete and exactly where it should be in its life cycle.*

Have you ever seen a flower that was not perfect? What made it *not perfect?* Nature made it the way it was. If it did not seem perfect to you, it is because you judged it relative to other flowers or otherwise decided that the flower was not the way you thought it should be. Notice that. Notice that even flowers seem flawed when people judge them. By people's standards, there are no "perfect" flowers, but by nature's standards, all flowers are perfect. Flowers fit perfectly into the world the way it is.

Can you see that the world is the way it is because people perceive it that way? If people could view the world as a perfect place to live, it would be perfect for them. If they could view themselves as perfect the way they are, they would *be* content, satisfied, and glad to be alive. But, of course, people see flaws and they conclude that there is something wrong with the world and themselves. Using nature's criteria, you are perfect as you are now. But, if you are like most people, you neither feel perfect nor like someone who has the power to create a perfect world.

We shall be discussing ways to grow more satisfied with yourself throughout the book. The goal is *not* to have you change so that you feel better about yourself. The goal is to feel better about yourself so that you will grow and change naturally. You have to play the game with the you that is here, now, not the you about whom you dream.

There are a couple of things you can do right now to become more self-satisfied. The first is to commit yourself to discovering what makes you unique and special. Second, you must begin keeping all your agreements with yourself. If you plan to start jogging, read more, or take time for yourself, you must live up to that commitment. When people do not keep their commitments to themselves, they begin to lose trust in themselves. Each broken agreement results in another cause for self-doubt, and that undermines self-confidence.

If you practice keeping your commitments diligently, you will develop self-trust, self-confidence, and self-satisfaction. Once you have learned to keep commitments to your Self, begin keeping your agreements with others and watch their trust in you grow. You must uphold all agreements such as:

Keeping your appointments.
Being on time.
Doing what you say you'll do.
Finishing what you say you'll finish.
And so on.

When you keep your commitments, notice how much more trust people have in you! But you can't *try* to keep your agreements — you must do it.

The happiness game calls for 100% committment and 100% participation. The more you hold back, the less you will get out of the game. I know, it's scary to take risks. It's hard to keep agreements. But what is harder still is playing the game with the brakes on. You have to go for it.

APPRECIATE WHAT YOU HAVE

The second objective of the happiness game is to appreciate fully what you have. My friends and I had everything for which we dreamed: health, education, family, home, car, money, and recognition. But something was missing. *Clearly, what was missing was the proper attitude.*

We thought that to be happy, we had to *have* things. So we did everything that had to be done to get those things. But in so doing, we gave up all time for fun and recreation.

We learned the hard way that happiness does not come from *having* more or *doing* something different. Happiness comes from appreciating fully everything we have and everything we do. Happiness, in other words, is living in the now and appreciating what we have now.

We shall be learning many techniques for developing the ability to live in the now. You can begin the lesson at this time, if you want. The first step is become aware of your thoughts. As you read through this book, notice how your mind reacts to each new idea. Notice how your mind wants to criticize, to evaluate, and to resist. Just notice it; don't try to do anything about it, yet.

Second, begin noticing what beliefs lie behind your thoughts. What do you believe is the *real* cause of happiness? How does that belief affect your acceptance of the definition of happiness used in this book? What are your beliefs about your self-worth? How do those beliefs get in your way of appreciating fully who you are? What are your beliefs about others and the way they feel about you? How do those beliefs govern how you act with others? What are your beliefs about your life thus far? How do those beliefs affect your ability to live a life full of joy and contentment? We shall be exploring your awareness skills and your belief patterns in more depth later. For now, you may want to practice this exercise:

1. Be aware of the thoughts that dominate your mind throughout the day. Notice what you think about when you awaken, what you think about as you're getting dressed, eating breakfast, driving, working, and resting. Some people believe you are what you think. What do *you* think?

2. Become more aware of the beliefs behind your thoughts. It may help to write down your most strongly held beliefs. For example, what do you believe about your personality? What do you believe about marriage? What do you believe about getting up in the morning? What do you believe about breakfast? What do you believe about your job?

3. Start making the connection between your beliefs and your experiences. For example, if you believe that breakfast is important, what happens when you skip breakfast? If you believe your job is boring, what happens at work? *If you believe you don't have enough money now, what happens when you try to feel satisfied? If you believe you need more of something to be happy, what happens when you seek contentment?* What thoughts came up in each instance?

APPRECIATE LIFE THE WAY IT IS

The third objective of the game is to appreciate life the way it is. You can choose life to be the way it is or you can wish it were different. If you choose to accept life the way it is, then life will be fine for you. If you wish life were different, you will be dissatisfied with the way it is. Another way of putting it is: Choose what you have and you'll always have what you choose; be dissatisfied with what you have and you'll always be dissatisfied.

Some people feel strongly about this concept. They are not willing to accept life as it is now, but they will be quite willing to accept life when it brings them joy and contentment. But joy and contentment never come to those who don't find it now! Those people who are addicted to needing more are never satisfied. What are your thoughts about addictions? What are the beliefs behind those thoughts? What would have to happen before you experienced joy? Do you believe that accepting things the way they are now will make you *stuck* where you are? Why couldn't you be joyful now and seek more joy later? The truth is that people who enjoy life now have more energy to move on because they don't dissipate their strength in worry, doubt, fear, anger, and jealousy.

My father was a success. He always had "enough." He worked happily because he enjoyed what he was doing. He followed where his natural inclinations led him, and that path led to success without struggle. Do you know people who truly love their work? They may work long hours, but work and fun for them are synonymous. They become successes because it is easy to work hard when work is fun.

You, too, can be happy now *and* be successful as well. Career choices make a big difference. The idea is to do what you enjoy; success comes easily when we are doing what we like because we like doing it for long hours. Watch a child playing hour after hour and you will see the inexhaustible energy that comes with doing what you like. Success and happiness are compatible if our beliefs don't interfere and tell us that certain careers are inherently "better" and doing what we like is not "right."

People waste an incredible amount of energy being upset and saying that "life is not right, life is not fair, and things should be different." That energy could be used constructively since we know that happy people have more energy. But that means being happy with *what is* now.

When I first became serious about happiness, I noticed that very young children usually live in the now. They quickly forget about the past. Thinking back, I remember how my friends and I enjoyed life as children. Even though there were some terrible moments when we were lonely or hurt, those moments passed quickly and each moment was a new experience. When did life change from a moment by moment experience to become a long, drawn out struggle to "succeed?"

For my friends and me, life changed by the time we were teenagers. Our childlike enthusiasm returned only occasionally — for a trip to the beach, to Disneyland, or some other "big event." We had learned to compare what was happening currently with past events that were more fun. We had also begun to anticipate future events. We were so busy thinking about the past or the future that we no longer enjoyed the *now*. Focusing on tomorrow, we lost today.

There are many adults who feel fortunate just to be alive. Some of them have just been in an accident and have lived on the brink of death. All their attentions were focused on one thing—surviving. For them, continuing to live was the most important goal in their lives. People who have been extremely ill and soldiers on an extremely dangerous mission have experienced the same feeling. Isn't it tragic that some of us need a life-threatening event in order to appreciate what we have now?

Although I have known many people who gained an appreciation of life by nearly dying, I have known other people who have experienced lesser shocks that opened their eyes to life. One very close friend was devastated when his wife left him. He had been drifting through life enjoying some days, not enjoying others, and generally not experiencing the aliveness that we call happiness. The shock of divorce shattered his world of complacency. He realized how good his life had been, even though he didn't recognize it at the time. And he realized that he could find happiness only through re-aligning his priorities and getting more out of what he had. This friend is currently playing the happiness game and his life is improving almost daily. He is learning that happiness can be developed, and that he must keep practicing happiness skills or risk falling back into despair. One of the biggest aids to his growth is the support he gets from friends.

CHOOSING PARTNERS FOR THE GAME

If you want to share the joy of playing the happiness game with others, you should understand that there are different levels of players who will approach the game differently. Although there could be an infinite number of player classifications, the following should help you select partners.

Professionals: These people have graduated from courses in Zen or similar kinds of awareness groups. These pros can handle all kinds of stressful situations with ease. They are pursuing states of complete harmony and bliss. They are likely to be beyond playing the happiness game. They will be pleased to hear you are beginning the quest, but they will not make interesting partners for you.

Intermediate Players: These players have graduated from courses in est, Lifespring, Cornucopia, Insight, gestalt, and other life education training courses or have read the self-help manuals and put the concepts into practice. They will understand the concepts of the game clearly and will be willing to share their experiences with you. Give them a copy of this book as a memento of their training and they will be quite pleased. The book will remind them of concepts they learned and introduce them to some new ones. These players will return the favor by helping you play the game and supporting you when it gets difficult. Don't be shy in asking them for advice.

Beginners: These people have read some of the self-help literature and understand the value of personal development courses. But few have put into practice the concepts they have learned. They make wonderful partners in the game because they are open to new experiences and will share their discoveries with you. Give them a copy of the book and get together with them periodically to discuss how it is going. A group of eight to ten is a good size for sharing the concepts together. The game is much easier to master with this kind of support.

Spectators: There are many people who do not seem interested in the happiness game. They feel perfectly content being observers rather than participants. Many of them are afraid to change their beliefs or their behavior for fear of the unknown. They are unlikely to respond favorably to pressure to join the game or share your experiences. Some of these people will never agree to play the game, but that's their choice and *that's OK*. Others will benefit greatly and need to be led gently and quietly into the game. Give them a copy of this book as a gift and do not mention it again for a while. Periodically, you might ask them if they enjoyed a chapter you found interesting. Be prepared for much resistance. Don't try to play the game with these people. Their negativism could be contagious. Simply be there if they need you and try to show them by example. They will join when they are ready.

Some concepts in the book are more difficult to understand than others and some are more difficult to implement in your life. Don't bother trying to fully understand each one at the first reading.

Simply read through the book, practice filling out the score sheeets, and notice how you feel. Later, discuss the ideas with others and share your experiences. The whole idea of having partners in the game is to have people who support your efforts at improving your happiness skills and who are willing to share their successes. The more partners you find, the more experiences you will share. Over time, you will see the value of each concept.

AN OVERVIEW OF THE GAME

Let's pause for a moment and look at the happiness game as a whole. *P. 15* That way we will know what we are doing and why. We can also anticipate what is coming next and prepare for it.

To play the happiness game well demands that you develop various skills. To play golf or tennis well, you must learn to concentrate on the ball, to keep your temper under control, to perform all the strokes well, to learn various strategies, to practice, to plan your games, and to give up your bad habits. Many of the same skills are required in the happiness game. These are the steps you will follow:

1. In Chapter One, we have learned the objectives of the game and how to select partners. You shall also have a chance to test how well you are playing the game now. From that base, you will learn how to play better.

2. To get the most out of a game, you need to schedule time to play it. Ideally, you schedule your days with a balance between work and play. That is the subject of Chapter Two.

3. You will learn to be more aware of your thoughts, feelings, beliefs, and addictions. You will understand what is keeping you from becoming a better player and how to conquer those barriers. Chapter Three will be devoted to exercises that will get you in shape for the happiness game.

THE HAPPINESS GAME

4. The next step in the game is to begin practicing techniques for becoming more outgoing, for controlling anger, and for being more self-assertive. You will also explore further the beliefs that prevent you from improving your game. This development of game skills is discussed in Chapters Four and Five.

5. Chapter Six deals with the factor that makes games fun for everyone. That fun factor is *enthusiasm*.

6. To many people, love is the most important thing in their life. Chapter Seven discusses the establishment and maintenance of loving relationships. Certainly, the game is more fun when it is played with others in love.

7. Chapter Eight introduces a whole new look to the game. Rather than playing the game for ourselves, we learn to play the game for others. There is no greater joy than recognizing the links between Self, others, and the environment and playing the game in that context.

8. Every game takes on a new dimension when we learn strategies for playing better. Chapter Nine introduces several such strategies.

9. When all the studying is over, you might want to move on to tougher opponents. Chapter Ten will introduce you to a few human potential groups that provide the atmosphere for playing the game on a professional level. This is supplementary to the happiness game. You won't need the groups because you will have learned all the happiness skills in this book. But they're available if you're interested.

EVALUATING YOUR PRESENT SELF

Before you begin warming up to play the happiness game, it might be instructive to learn how the scoring works and to see what kind of player you are. Here's how the scoring will go throughout the book. I will give you a list of ten statements. You should read each one carefully and decide how accurately that statement describes you. You will then give yourself a score from 1 to 10. A *10* indicates you feel the statement describes you perfectly. A *1* indicates you feel it doesn't describe you at all. For example, the statement might be "I rarely worry." If you're worried much of the time, give yourself a 2 or 3. But, if you feel content most of the time, give yourself a score of 9 or 10.

There are no measures to use when determining your score other than *your feelings.* You keep score only to reveal to yourself where you are now and how much progress you have made over time. You should not compare scores with others because that could lead to all kinds of "I'm better than you are" games.

OK, let's start. Read each of the following statements and score yourself from 1 to 10 depending on how accurately *you feel* the statement describes you — 1 means the statement does not describe you at all, 10 means it describes you perfectly.

Where Are You Now?

Statement	Now	After 6 Months	After 1 Year
1. I am basically a happy person.	_____	_____	_____
2. I feel satisfied with who I am.	_____	_____	_____
3. My life is great the way it is.	_____	_____	_____
4. I have a balance between work and play.	_____	_____	_____
5. I am self-confident.	_____	_____	_____
6. I love myself and others.	_____	_____	_____
7. I handle anger, fear, and doubt well.	_____	_____	_____
8. I know what I want in life.	_____	_____	_____
9. I have good self-control.	_____	_____	_____
10. I feel successful.	_____	_____	_____
Total Scores	_____	_____	_____
Starting Date	_____		

Chapter 2

Scheduling the Game

*T*he problem with most of us is that we simply don't have enough time to be playing many games, including the happiness game. To find the time to play, we would have to do some careful planning. We would have to schedule the game at a time that was convenient. So let's take a few minutes to plan when the best times would be for playing the game.

Busy people need to schedule periods when they can relax and have fun. This chapter discusses techniques for getting *more* out of every day through planning. More what? More of everything: fun, productivity, and relaxation. *The primary goal is to bring a better balance into life by scheduling more time for pleasure.* This does not mean making work or school less important; it simply means putting them into perspective so that they become part of, not replacements for, the happiness game.

My friends and I were good at making plans. We laid out elaborate plans for college and careers. We planned each day so that we could accomplish as much as possible. Happily, most of our plans came true. The reason is simple: Planning works!

Most people have learned the value of planning, but few of us have learned how to apply planning skills to getting more enjoyment out of life. The concept is simple, but the application is difficult. Often most people plan their life around work. If a person has planned a two week vacation and is suddenly called back because of something "important" at work, the vacation may get delayed or cancelled. On the other hand, very few people will delay or cancel going to work because they have an "important" need for a vacation.

It is clear that most people put work before pleasure. Students often put school before pleasure, although some parents would debate that point. What is not debatable is that both work and pleasure are enhanced by planning.

HOPING OR DREAMING IS NOT PLANNING

One of the major obstacles to finding more joy in the game of life is relying on hopes and dreams. There is a saying in basketball that "He sent up a prayer." This means that a player threw the ball toward the basket and prayed it would go in rather than concentrating on making a good shot. Such shots usually miss. Hoping and dreaming will not win a game. Most of us have learned that the hard way!

The world is full of wishers. No doubt you have heard them say:

I wish I could play tennis better.
I wish I had more friends.
I wish I knew how to ski.
I wish I read more.
I wish I had more money.

Wishes may not come true, but planned events do. So stop wishing and start planning.

My friend Tom wanted to ski more frequently. Every year at the end of the ski season, Tom would say, "Next year, I'm going to ski more often." The next year would come and Tom would think about skiing all winter but would never make concrete plans to go. One year, Tom sat down and set up a *plan.* He picked the exact dates that he would like to ski, called the ski resorts and made arrangements, and called the airlines for reservations. Tom *planned* to go skiing, and, sure enough, he went skiing where and when he wanted.

What do you wish for? More travel? Better skill at some sport? Even something as basic as *having more fun each day* takes careful planning. Since everyone would like to have more fun, let's use that goal as an example.

First, determine what is fun for you. Then *plan* to do whatever it is you enjoy for some time every day. For instance, if you want to read a good book, set aside some time each day and *plan* to read the book. Plan to take tennis lessons and you'll take them. Plan to have more people over and you'll have more people over. Be specific. Set a date. Set a time. *Write it down!* By planning a little happiness into each day, you will automatically put more happiness into your life.

THE HAPPINESS GAME

17

One day a student came to my office to discuss his grades. I noticed that he sometimes came late to class and often missed class entirely. I asked him, "What are you doing that causes you to be late and miss class?" His answer, "Nothing. I sometimes sleep too late and other times I just goof around." Can you imagine wasting the potentially most rewarding years of your life — the college years — doing nothing but "goofing around" and not enjoying it? I asked this student what he enjoyed doing best. He said he loved basketball and usually played all day on Saturday.

Right that minute, he and I planned a different kind of schedule. He planned to play a little basketball every morning as an incentive to get him out of bed and functioning. We then planned some time for study and some time with his friends. For the first time in years, this student looked forward to getting up in the morning. He rarely missed class after that and he was never late. His wishes for better grades and greater happiness came true with just a few minutes of planning.

There is more to the happiness game than planning, but planning is an excellent tool. Happiness tends to be an elusive goal; it takes constant awareness of the here and now and much day to day progress. But people did not get to the moon by wishing on a star or hoping for a scientific breakthrough. They got there by careful planning, dedicating themselves to the job, and, most of all, believing that it could be done.

BASING PLANS ON PAST PLEASURES

To plan for more joy in your life, it is important to know what has given you joy in the past.

Why not take a few minutes right now and review what has increased your joy in the past? When was your life fun and peaceful and you found it easy to smile? For example, some things that I really enjoy are:

Canoeing down a river on a warm, sunny summer day.

Lying on the beach with the sun on my back, watching the people go by.

Taking a nap in the middle of the afternoon.

Visiting friends and talking about what's fun in their lives.

Going back home to Ohio to visit my family.

Taking lazy rides in the country on a motorcycle.

Playing tennis with my wife and friends.

Talking about self-development programs and what they mean to me. (That's why I'm enjoying writing this book).

Listening to music.

Reading a book just for fun (as opposed to reading academic journals).

Going to funny movies and good plays.

Sitting with my son on my lap and talking.

Singing with my family and friends.

Walking through the woods and by a mountain stream.

Reading the human potential literature.

Just being alive in this most fascinating of times.

WHAT DO YOU ENJOY?

Take about ten minutes, if you will, and write down the things that you enjoy.

THINGS I ENJOY DOING

_____

_____

_____

THE HAPPINESS GAME

19

_____

_____

_____

_____

_____

_____

_____

THINGS I DO NOT ENJOY DOING

_____

_____

_____

_____

_____

_____

_____

_____

_____

_____

_____

What else do you enjoy? As you think of things, add them to your list until you have several pages.

Now here is a tough question: How much of your day do you spend doing the things you have listed? If you answer most of the day, then I should be reading your book. How do you do it? If you answer a small percentage of each day, join the crowd. Most of us spend the bulk of our days doing things we do not particularly like — things like work; watching TV programs we really do not enjoy; talking with people we really do not enjoy; fighting traffic to and from work; or performing household chores we find boring.

One way to become more joyful is to do more of the things we enjoy and less of the things we do not enjoy. "Easier said than done," you say. You are absolutely right, but it may not be as hard as you imagine. All it takes is planning.

PLANNING FOR FUN

Most of us do not do much planning for fun. Instead, we plan our work schedule, we plan our careers, and we plan for meeting our bills. Oh sure, we plan our vacations, but too often such plans detail where to go, when and how, but include few details about fun things to do. For example, have you ever found yourself racing to get to a vacation spot, annoyed at the traffic, fighting with the kids, just because you planned to be at some vacation stop at a particular time? You see, we often ruin our vacations because we planned *being places* rather than relaxing, taking our time, enjoying here, enjoying now. "We'll have fun tomorrow at the beach," often precludes having fun now. What if it rains tomorrow? No Fun?

Planning for happiness means *planning to live in the now every moment of your life.* For example, if you're driving to your vacation, you should enjoy the *now* scenery, the *now* freedom from work, the *now* closeness with family, the *now* sights, sounds and discoveries. Living in the now and planning are not inconsistent. Sometimes the best, most enjoyable thing to do *now* is to plan for the future.

THE HAPPINESS GAME

21

DAILY PLANS

Every day we need to find time to play the happiness game even though we may give primary attention to the work game, the child-rearing game, or another important game. The way to find time for fun during the day is to *plan* it into the day's schedule.

A good way to get more control over a day's activities is to take time the night before and list everything that you want to get done. Include in that list some fun things from the list you just prepared. Now put the items into some priority by placing a (1) next to high priority items, a (2) next to less critical items, and a (3) next to items that can be delayed if necessary. For example, a report due in two days might be given a (1). A budget due in three weeks would get a (2). Things like washing the car and mowing the lawn, etc. might get a (3). Fun events always get a (1) or (2). For example, you could schedule 20 minutes in the morning for meditation. You could schedule 30 minutes at lunch for jogging or reading a book. You could schedule an hour or more in the evening for working on your hobby or exercizing or enjoying a leisurely meal. Such planning assures a minimum of two hours a day that are yours to play the happiness game. Of course, you can schedule much more play time if you want.

Put all the items on a piece of paper in the order of importance. Do the most important items during the time of day when you are most alert. Then scratch that item off the list. This is an important step. Crossing out items as you go along gives you a feeling of accomplishment and control. It also keeps the list handy so you can check what is next. There is no time wasted trying to remember what to do next — most of that work is done the night before.

Some people are morning people and would do number (1) priority items first thing in the morning. Some people simply don't function until 11:00 A.M. or so. Such people could schedule low priority things in the morning, scratch them off the list, and clear the mind for high priority work from 11:00 until the task is completed. Lunch comes when hunger comes, not at noon. Some slow starters find early morning jogging or other exercise gets their blood flowing must faster and eliminates the early morning blahs.

It is easier to work hard knowing that there are priority times set aside for fun later. "Work hard and play later" is a good motto to follow. But "play hard and work later" is equally good. Experiment until you find a pattern that suits your own needs.

Have you ever written down your daily tasks like this? If you have, you know the benefits already: fewer forgotten tasks, more control, more accomplishment, more time (less wasted wondering what to do next), and more happiness. If you have never done this, you will be amazed at the effectiveness of this little exercise. But you must keep at it. If you let it slip, you will find yourself buried in work and confused as to what to do first. And what usually gets pushed way to the back is *fun*.

But remember if circumstances change during the day, plans should change as well. That calls for re-doing your list, realigning the priorities, but keeping happiness games high on the list.

At the end of the day, review your list. Items not completed should be listed for the next day. Some low priority items might rise to the number (1) spot. For example, the lawn may be threatening to return to the forest if not done today. So, give lawn cutting a (1) priority, schedule it when appropriate, and plan the rest of the day accordingly.

I have found something very interesting doing this daily planning. Sometimes when I schedule something fun like a game of tennis, I receive a call asking me to do something else, like work or volunteer at church. I find that having a priority list enables me to say, "I'm busy then, would some other time be convenient?" You know what? Others don't plan their days as well, so they usually adapt to you. But you have to stick to your priorities. If you can't take on more, say so!

When you feel really burdened by the tasks you must accomplish, what should you do first? Take a ten minute break and write a priority list, put the items in order and do first things first. And be sure to schedule time for fun. All work and no play is all work and no play. Every day consists of 1,440 minutes. Schedule a few of them for happiness and fun.

LIFETIME PLANS

Once you have mastered time on a daily basis, you are ready to tackle life's long-range plans. What would you like to accomplish in your life? Why not *put happiness first?* Now, what is second, third, fourth, and fifth? Would you like to have many friends and make lots of money? List your goals and then list what you need to reach those goals. Then break down the list of what you need to do into yearly goals, monthly goals, weekly goals, and daily goals. For example, if you would like to lose 10 pounds, make your goal realistic and give yourself a year to do it. That is about a pound a month (minus the holiday season when losing weight usually becomes a low priority). A pound a month is a reasonable, maintainable goal. On your daily planning list, you would include a diet goal that would vary by circumstances, but would always lead to a loss of one pound per month. Easy and effective.

CHANGING PLANS

Surprisingly, many people follow their plans *too closely.* This is surprising because plans are supposed to be good. But note what happens. A young man decides he wants to be an engineer. He enrolls in college and is in his third year when he suddenly realizes that he is not suited for engineering. But he has invested three years of college in engineering, so rather than doing what he wants, he plugs along until he finishes. He may even pursue a career in engineering. But all his life he may never really enjoy his work. What went wrong? He made plans and stuck to them even though it became obvious that the goal was not right for him.

How many people do you know who are "stuck" in jobs or home situations that they do not like? What is holding them there? — plans made years ago. People sometimes become slaves to plans. If they plan to be one place for three days and another place for five, they stay three days at the first place *regardless!* They then go to the other place for *five* days — no more, no less. Where is the flexibility that allows for more fun?

But notice also the current trend toward breaking lifetime plans. Men and women are quitting promising careers to pursue less lucrative but more rewarding (happier) careers. They have always realized that happiness is more important than money, but have put off choosing happiness until late in their careers. Finally, they have seen the light, hooray for them!

Are you stuck with commitments you made to yourself or others? Are they keeping you from joy and happiness? Then why not break them? Because it is "wrong" to break commitments? We all make mistakes and some mistakes involve commitments. This is inevitable. We are sincere when we make commitments to jobs, friends, and family, but sometimes circumstances change. When they do, our plans must change as well. What is the major criterion for change? — greater overall joy for all concerned. Of course, we should never blindly chase happiness or joy and hurt others along the way. On the other hand, we should never *blindly* follow a *plan* hurting ourselves along the way. Follow the rule of reason, weigh the benefits and costs, and choose the plan with the greater happiness for all.

EXERCISES FOR PLANNING MORE FUN IN YOUR LIFE

Success is achieved by planning for more time, more fun, and more success. Practicing this exercise will help you reach that goal:

1. *Write* down on a sheet of paper all the things you enjoy doing.
2. *Write* down your lifetime goals for your career, your relationships, travel, etc.
3. *Write* down everything you have always hoped for in life.
4. Begin today to plan for a better tomorrow. Do that by listing everything you have to do at work and at home. Then list everything you would like to do for fun.
5. Put all your tasks in order of priority, assigning a (1) to top priority items, a (2) to less important items, and a (3) to items that can be postponed. Then list your fun items in the same order of priority, but be sure to assign them (1)s and (2)s. Then combine the lists.
6. Schedule work and play priorities at effective times throughout the day.
7. Be flexible in your scheduling so you don't feel controlled by your plans. If you must put off having fun, give it double time and a higher priority the next day.
8. Make a calendar where you schedule monthly and yearly events that will eventually give you all the lifetime experiences you desire.
9. Commit yourself to keeping your agreements and writing down your goals daily. Do what you *want* to do and you will have the energy to complete all your tasks.
10. Catch yourself whenever you express a wish and turn it into a plan by scheduling it for a specific date and time.

Scheduling the Game

26

DOING WHAT YOU WANT

As a professor at a large eastern university, I am exposed to thousands of students every year. After years of working with these students and talking with people of all ages and all income brackets, some facts have become clear to me: many people have little or no idea what they want out of life, many people do not enjoy their jobs, and many people do not know what to do about it. It is also clear that most people have a rather clear concept of what they do *not* like and almost everyone has something they like to do.

Planning your life might begin, therefore, by completing the list of things that you do not like to do and things you do like to do. Begin improving your life by discontinuing most of the things you don't like to do. Some things will take tremendous will power, but the sense of accomplishment will more than compensate. Do you smoke even though you would prefer not to? Do you drink beer at parties when you would really prefer orange juice? Do you eat too much and regret it later? Do you visit people you would rather not see? What are some of the things you do that you would rather not do? Why are you doing them? What would it take to stop? Are you ready to do that?

An interesting exercise to determine what is really important to you is to answer this question in writing: "If I knew I would be struck dead by lightening six months from today, what would I do until then?" By answering this question, you will find what you really value in life, what your priorities are, and how to find time to accomplish your high priority objectives.

To see what you value in life, pretend your home is burning down. You have two minutes to take what is dearest to you: your spouse, your kids, money, a manuscript, etc. What would you grab? What if you would get severely burned doing that? Would you still pursue your plan? Now look again at what you chose and see if it brings you joy. These exercises are valuable for getting clear about life and what it would take for you to make the most of it.

THE HAPPINESS GAME

DOING WHAT IS RIGHT FOR YOU

There are times in our lives when the greatest need is to "get away from it all" and to do nothing for a while. Most of us never satisfy that need for fear that we cannot afford the time or money or because we regard that desire as irresponsible.

Some of us do give in to such feelings, but because of guilt, never fully appreciate the benefits from such a break. Times when these feelings are likely to occur are when you graduate from high school or college or are divorced or widowed. The pressures from a long period of mental stress are over and you are not psychologically ready for attacking the new life that awaits you.

There is nothing wrong with doing nothing! But if you choose to do nothing, like take a prolonged vacation, you must accept that decision fully and not worry about obligations or money. It is better not to take such a break until you are truly prepared to free your mind from the everyday cares of the world. Given such preparation, you can use the break to cleanse your system of petty cares, past mistakes, and personal misfortunes.

When you decide to do something, you should do it right! Work hard, play hard, and relax hard. Halfway measures bring halfway results. And you have to trust your own feelings and do what is right for you. In short, even doing nothing takes lots of planning and care. After doing nothing for a while, you will recapture your natural enthusiasm for actively playing the game of life. You will attack your job with renewed vigor and do well.

When the need for doing nothing strikes again, plan for it, do it, and then return again to whatever you do in life. Use these words of wisdom from Cicero for a guide: "He does not seem to me to be a free man who does not sometimes do nothing."

TIMING YOUR UPS AND DOWNS

Some people are night people and others are morning people. To be most productive, we should keep track of our daily rhythms and plan our most challenging tasks when we are most mentally alert. A day in spring may find you more awake and full of pep than that same day in the heart of the summer.

Scientists today are very interested in biorhythms. They have found that people go through cycles where their moods and physical abilities decline, then peak again in a regular pattern over time. People vary slightly in their patterns, but everyone seems to follow a cycle of "ups" and "downs." To test this theory, you need only record your "downs." You are likely to find they occur regularly. You might want to keep track of physical well-being and mental states separately. All patterns may not be the same.

Once you have established which hours are best for you, which days, which months, and have charted your biorhythms, you are ready to plan your activities. Plan to schedule your most important projects during your most productive periods. Notice if you have a down period after major holidays like Christmas and New Years. Note also those times when you invariably feel like taking a vacation. You will find regular patterns that provide clear guidelines for work, major projects, vacations, and so on.

BALANCING WORK WITH PLAY

The old saying, "All work and no play makes Jack a dull boy," is certainly true for many people. You must know people who are "workaholics." In these times of dog-eat-dog living, there are millions of men and women in the United States who have high blood pressure, who work long hours, and who literally don't know how to relax. These people may work themselves to death if they don't follow the goalsetting procedures and priority-setting techniques outlined here.

Some people need a friend or even a professional consultant to come in and plan their day with them. Workaholics are just as sick in their own way as alcoholics who walk the streets doing nothing. Both are ruining their lives and most likely the lives of their families. Both need help!

The busier you are the more critical it becomes that you take time during the day to review priorities, plan the remainder of the day, and rest. Many people are suprised by the feeling of control they can have over their time when they make daily schedules.

Women who work at home also find their hectic schedules become more manageable if each day has a plan. Sometimes children and emergencies raise havoc with plans, but these interruptions call for *more* frequent planning sessions, not fewer. Everyone needs time for themselves, and that time is available *if* it is given priority over other matters. We must be firm about maintaining priority schedules, or we'll soon lose control over our lives. Only with control can we be truly happy.

SCORING THE GAME

How well are you scheduling fun in your day now? Score yourself from 1 to 10 depending on how accurately you feel the following statements describe you — 1 means the statement does not describe you at all, 10 means it describes you perfectly.

HOW MUCH TIME DO YOU GIVE TO HAPPINESS

Statements	Now	After 6 Months	1 Year
1. I rarely say "I wish I could do something;" instead, I plan for it and do it.	_____	_____	_____
2. I write down all my plans for fun.	_____	_____	_____
3. I have listed all the things in life that give me pleasure so I can plan to do them more often and I have listed all the things in life I don't particularly enjoy so I can plan to do them less often.	_____	_____	_____
4. I set aside some time each day to plan the next day's activities.	_____	_____	_____
5. I give enjoyable things priority in may daily plans.	_____	_____	_____
6. I have clear lifetime plans and know what I must do this year to accomplish those plans.	_____	_____	_____

...continued

THE HAPPINESS GAME

7. I am not stuck doing what I'm doing because I'm afraid to change plans at this stage of my life. _____ _____ _____

8. I can do nothing all day and not feel guilty. _____ _____ _____

9. I balance work with play and give each about equal priority. _____ _____ _____

10. I know fully that having some fun every day will not get in my way of doing well at school or at work. _____ _____ _____

Total Scores _____ _____ _____

Starting Date _____

Chapter 3

Warming Up

*J*ust as it's important to warm up before jogging or playing tennis, it's also important to warm up before playing the happiness game. One of the most important warm up exercises is learning to control your mind rather than having it control you. Have you ever tried to do something, like balancing your checkbook, with someone making suggestions, criticizing, and generally being a nuisance? It can drive you crazy. Someone just like that is watching every move you make while you play the happiness game. That someone is your mind. Your mind will be sitting just above your shoulders interfering, being critical, and generally getting in your way of experiencing life. To win the game, you need to manage that nagging background noise.

One way of managing your mind is to keep it in the now. Your mind should not be dwelling on what happened in the past nor longing for the future, unless you want it to! You can certainly use the past as a guide to the future and plan for the future. But *you,* not your mind, should decide where and when this occurs. Often your mind will drift away like it is a separate entity from yourself. That is quite normal. We shall learn to control that wandering so that your mind works with you rather than apart from you.

MIND AWARENESS

Have you stopped to notice that voice in your head that talks *at* you all day long? That voice is the voice of your mind. It is the defender of your belief system.

We have said that one goal of the happiness game is to appreciate fully who you are now. Typically, that voice in the background will be saying "You can't be happy with who you are now. You are not good enough yet. You are not successful enough yet. You will grow lazy if you accept yourself as you are." To win the happiness game requires getting control over that negative voice. That voice must be trained to be supportive or, at the minimum, stay out of the way.

Do you feel you have control over your thoughts (that voice)? Can you stop thinking? The answer is you *can* learn to control your mind and to program it with positive thoughts. But first you have to become more aware of what your mind is doing.

Often when I am reading or talking with someone, my mind will wander off on some other subject. Such mind trips used to annoy me. But now I enjoy being aware of the tricks my mind is playing. I know that I *can* bring it back.

Take a day or two and listen intently to that voice in your head. Notice what it says. Does it tend to judge others by the way they look,

Warming Up

34

by their success, by their sex, by their race, or by their education? What does it say about politicians? About policemen? What does your voice say about the economic conditions today? About the prospects for world peace? How does it react when others criticize you? How often does it say "This isn't right, this isn't fair, things should be different"? What beliefs are behind those thoughts?

After you have listened for a few days to your inner voice, you will know what you are up against. You will see that your mind holds prejudices, conclusions, beliefs, and concepts that, if accepted, will prevent personal growth. To win the happiness game, you may have to give up some beliefs, like being right about the way you judge things.

Notice the voice while you play a competitive game. When I am playing tennis, my voice keeps saying things like "Oh no, that one is coming to your backhand, you are going to miss it!" or "Keep your eyes on the ball, stupid!" That voice keeps a constant chatter in my head that often distracts me from my game.

What does your voice say about you? What does it say about the way you sing, about your intelligence, about your personality?

Most "voices" are very critical of things. Is yours? The major goal of the mind is survival, and your mind thinks survival depends upon maintaining your beliefs. It might sacrifice anything, including your joy and your body, to be right. You could literally die if you let your mind keep you from becoming aware of a healthier, happier way of living. To win the happiness game, you must learn to quiet that voice and to break through the mental barriers that keep you from seeing a more joyful path through life.

CONTROLLING THE MIND

What does it feel like to be free of that voice in your head? Have you ever noticed how content you feel when the babbling ends? Most people shut off their "voice" subconciously. They do it regularly, but not purposely. Some do it through jogging, reading, gardening, or listening to music. Others play games that take concentration. Still others stare at the waves coming in off the ocean or at mountain vistas. In each case, the person concentrates so thoroughly and naturally that mind babble is cut off. What emerges is a naturally happy Self.

Notice that Self next time you concentrate on your hobby or favorite sport. If I were to stop you in the middle of your task and ask you how you were at that moment, you are likely to say "I feel fine and everything else is fine, thank you." That, of course, is the definition of happiness — feeling fine with "what is" now.

Now you know a very easy technique for controlling your mind when it begins to send out negative signals. Simply *get involved* in something fun that takes *total* concentration and your mind will become so absorbed in the effort that it will leave you alone. You feel at peace with your Self and at peace with the world. That is the *experience* of happiness.

WARM-UP EXERCISES
FOR CONTROLLING YOUR MIND

1. Commit yourself 100% to *be* a happy person.
2. Learn what happiness is — the ability to appreciate fully *who you are, what you have, and life as it is now.*
3. Notice what causes your unhappiness — it's that "voice" in your head saying now is not good enough.
4. Practice shutting off that voice by concentrating on your favorite activity. Notice the feeling of calm and satisfaction that occurs when you do concentrate.
5. Visualize your favorite spot and everything that normally occurs. (If you are not able to concentrate on your favorite scene or activity because you are not physically able to, simply close your eyes and go through the whole process mentally. If your activity is boating, imagine walking down the dock, climbing into the

boat, starting the engine or raising the sails, and begin drifting away from the dock and go on a trip. The results are the same whether you actually go boating or do it in your mind: Your mind does not distinguish between real events and imagined events when it tells the body to relax.)

6. Experience the contentment that results from this exercise so you know what happiness is. From this *Values* base, you can build a life of fun, joy, and excitement.

TRANSCENDENTAL MEDITATION

An effective and popular technique for clearing the mind of its constant babble is Transcendental Meditation (TM). Many people have the idea that TM is some kind of religious practice. But TM is merely a mental exercise that has many of the same effects as a long nap: relaxation, energy, and awareness. We have noted that one means for clearing the mind is to concentrate on something. In TM, that something is called a mantra. A mantra is a word or a sound. For example, one could repeat the word "one" over and over, drawing out the sound — O N N N N N N E. You are given your own personal mantra the day you are initiated into TM. The TM instructor places great emphasis on the proper selection of the mantra each person uses.

The concept of TM is more important than details. The idea is to quiet your "voice" by concentrating on something. The object of your concentration could be a candle flame, a beautiful scene, a word, almost anything. TM recommends that a person concentrate 20 minutes twice a day, in the morning and in the early evening.

Once the mind is relaxed, a person can become more aware of

his or her surroundings. Meditation helps people see things more clearly, to be more open, and to be more relaxed. That is, the mind transcends its normal functioning. It enters a new level of consciousness.

One part of the happiness game is to explore your world for those things that *naturally* draw your attention. I have found, for example, complete relaxation and clarity sitting on our deck looking at the woods. The sounds of the breeze, the birds and the ducks on the pond act as a powerful tranquilizer. Concentrating on this scene takes no effort and has the effect of a mantra for me. Variety is important to maintain interest, so one should concentrate, relax, and later focus on something else. For example, I sometimes go to the ocean and concentrate on the waves. Such concentration for twenty minutes is easy, and I feel happy and content. Often people *try* to concentrate, but that is a mistake. Effective concentration comes from a relaxed, sustained interest in something naturally attractive.

JOGGING AS MEDITATION

Another fast growing meditation technique today is jogging. Joggers who set out to improve their physical state found to their surprise that the mental effects were as great or greater. Jogging for a half-hour or more forces one to establish a certain natural rhythm. One *concentrates* on running, silences the voice, and opens the mind to new experiences. The result is an altered state of consciousness, a certain mental relaxation, increased awareness, and a feeling of well-being. Many people find it hard to start a jogging program. You know why? Their inner voice keeps telling them that they are not the type, that they are too tired, that they are hurting, and so on. Joggers who fight their inner voice's constant harrassment and manage to get up to twenty minutes or more of running finally break through the bondage of their mind. They relax and find jogging much easier. The body is willing; in fact, the body often needs exercise desperately, but the mind is weak and resistive. To become a jogger, therefore, is a mental as much as a physical struggle.

What do you do to quiet your mind? Some people don't know until they think about it for a while, as we shall see below.

CONCENTRATION IN ACTION

Buzz and his son simply could not reach an agreement over who would mow the lawn. Contrary to most people's experience, it was Buzz, the father, who insisted that he be allowed to mow the lawn rather than his son. Why? Was it too dangerous using the riding mower? Was his son too young? The answer surprised Buzz as much as anybody. After some discussion, he suddenly became more aware of the feeling of peace he got while mowing. Furthermore, he found that he got tremendous insight into many of his problems during that time. He seemed to have an "altered state of consciousness."

Buzz did not know why he loved mowing the lawn until he learned about meditation; he just knew that he *experienced* calm and awareness doing it, and that experience felt good. It was a feeling of being in control and being in the now.

What do you do that results in such an experience? It could be gardening, listening to music, sitting by a babbling brook, reading, watching the sunset, or any of hundreds of other experiences. Next time you do it, notice how you feel. Notice that answers to problems seem to appear from nowhere. Notice how easy it is to smile, to sigh and let the tension out, and to be — dare I say it? — happy. Then use that experience over and over as detailed in the exercise.

YOU CREATE YOUR OWN REALITY

Your belief system distorts your view of the world. What you see is filtered through your attitudes and your biases so that your world supports your conclusions. Most people say of things, "I'll believe it when I see it." But seeing is not believing if what you see is distorted or unclear. On the other hand, the happiness game is based on the premise: "You'll *see* it when you *believe* it!" You will see a you that is self-confident and joyful when you believe you are such a person. You'll see that you have enough now when you believe you do. You'll see the world as perfect as it is when you believe it is.

- You See It When You "Values-Vision" It ....

You create your own reality. Right now your reality may not appear to be all you would like it to be. You could try to change the circumstances, change how others behave, and change the political, economic, social, and legal systems so that they pleased you. *Or you could change yourself so that you're happy with life as it is now.* Which path do you feel is easier? Is your mind telling you that you *have to* choose the harder path because things simply *must be changed?* Are you addicted to being responsible for recreating the world according to your standards? What are your beliefs about the reality of that goal? Does that mean that this world is hopeless? It is, if you believe it is. But it could be a world full of wonder and magic and fulfillment if you believed that. The choice is yours.

✓ "Values-Visioned" It ....

Imagine this situation. You are leaving later than you planned for a fantastic new play in town. You get in your car and discover you have a flat tire. There is no other car available and you are staying at a home with no phone. What are your options?

- You could get angry and upset.
- You could change the tire and arrive late.
- You could run to the neighbors and borrow their car or call a cab.
- You could go back in the house and enjoy doing something else.
- You could hitch a ride.
- You could try to drive with the flat tire.

I could list 1,000 different options you could create for yourself given the same event. But many of those experiences would be unavailable if you were addicted to have things work the way you would like. Would you *have* to get to the play if you had tickets? What addiction is that? Would you *have* to be on time? Could you simply turn around, go back in the house, and enjoy a good game of chess? Would your mind let you?

The moral of the story is this: Every event in your life offers you a new opportunity to create happiness in your life. Every event can be viewed from many different angles. The event could result in anger, fear, worry, doubt, and other negative feelings. Or it could result in an opportunity for growth, and an opportunity for happiness. The choice is yours if you are the manager of your mind.

STOPPING THE OLD MIND GAMES

Another warm-up exercise is to notice the games our minds are playing now. It is one thing to get the mind to relax and be content with what is. It is another to be actively involved with life and to play relaxed. One thing that keeps us tense is our competitiveness. Let's explore what happens when our minds play the "winning" game.

When I became clear about the relationship between success and happiness, I felt I had overcome a major hurdle in my life. But behind that hurdle was an even bigger hurdle called "winning." I was addicted to winning. I needed to win tennis games and debates; I needed to be right (and consequently make others wrong); and I needed to win friends. I really liked to win. If I couldn't win, then I wanted to "look good." I hated to look clumsy or dumb. Sometimes I would not try my hardest so I had an excuse for losing. My mind periodically had such a lock on me that I was totally under its domination. There was only one thing wrong with my addiction to winning — when I lost, I felt awful. I was filled with hate, embarrassment, and fear.

I guess it all started when I was a child. I was small for my age and bigger children would try to push me around. I vowed at a very young age never to let that happen. I fought every big guy on the block, in school, and in the Army. When I got too old to fight physically, I learned to fight intellectually. I would win by being smarter, and better prepared. I was often a wise guy, but my mind kept telling me I had to win *or else.*

The problem is that *needing* to win and to "be right" gets in the way of my happiness. I am trying to change that need to a *preference.* If I prefer to win, I can play and lose and still be happy. I can try hard, but I can relax and enjoy what I'm doing because I'm not addicted to winning. Not only am I happier, but my friends are happier as well. Occasionally my mind nags me, and once in a while I revert to my old "win at all costs" behavior.

One day I was discussing this concept with my class. I said that it is not important to win, and if it is important, it is only important to your belief system. I asked the class to examine how they felt about winning and to notice whether the need to win got in the way of their happiness.

Right after class, a student came to my office. She was a member of an intramural volleyball team and it was very important for her to win. She said that some of the players did not care whether they won or lost and they always "messed up practice." They would "waste the time meant for improving skills." My student felt like telling them, "You don't take this seriously, you horses' tails." I told her that they could rightfully reply, "You take this seriously, you horse's tail." She thought about that for a moment and asked "If winning isn't important, why keep score?" I explained that winning is fun and certainly something to try for, but not something to which you become addicted. "You know you need it if you become angry when you get behind. You know you are addicted if losing makes you unhappy. But why ruin the now fun of PLAYING a game by being so serious about winning it?"

I noted that this woman was serious about her grades and serious about being a success, so I asked her, "Is there anything in life you are not serious about? Do you do anything just for fun — with no need to be better or to win?" The woman thought for a moment and began to cry. She realized for the first time in her life that she was addicted to winning and that she could not do anything for fun. But such awareness is 70% of the cure.

On day I was walking to my office when I noticed a woman with a huge smile on her face. Her inner glow was apparent from quite a distance. Then I noticed that the woman was the student in my class who had seemed so serious before. She had been practicing for six months what we had discussed. She still tried very hard at volleyball and other games, but she had made winning a preference. She found that she played much better when she controlled her mind and concentrated on the game. The pressure was off, she was relieved, and her playing improved. By letting up on herself, she became *more* productive and much, much happier. *It is not important to win to be happy.*

Next time you play a competitive game, try setting a different goal. To win you have to stay relaxed, enjoy the competition, and have fun. You lose if you become upset when you make mistakes, swear, lose your temper, or cheat. The game score means nothing. The contest is between you and your mind and every point becomes another chance to win the happiness game. Every point is a new "event" that gives you an opportunity to choose relaxation, joy, self-control and fun *or* tenseness, competitiveness, anger, fear, and doubt. You will be amazed at how often you will win the game when you win the mind game. Try it and see. But remember, the competition from your mind may be tougher than you think.

THE HAPPINESS GAME

HAPPINESS AS A PRIMARY GOAL

Why is it that our minds are so eager to defend success and winning as primary goals? Are you willing to give up success and winning? (If so, you can still achieve success *and* win *and* have fun doing so, but such things will come naturally, not as a burden.)

Are you willing to defend the goal of happiness so forcefully? If not, why not? What is wrong with happiness in your belief system?

These are the kind of questions you should ask yourself as you go through this book. I know since I ask them of myself over and over, and it helps.

Happiness should be the primary goal in all your games; that includes the career game, athletic games, and so on. If your goal is success, you are likely to reach success and lose happiness in the search. That is what happens with the "I'll be happy when ..." game.

THE "I'LL BE HAPPY WHEN ...." GAME

People who are unhappy now often believe that the reason for their unhappiness is a lack of something. They believe they'll be happy when they have more money, when they have more time, or when they have more power. All the "I'll be happy when..." games can be fun to play, but they don't necessarily lead to happiness. In fact, they often lead to discontent and unhappiness. I began putting this in perspective when I read the following:

> *The more successful a person is in making money, collecting skills and possessions, developing exciting sexual relationships, acquiring knowledge and degrees, and achieving positions of status, power, and prestige, the less loving, peaceful, and contented he may find himself or herself.*

Warming Up

*And yet it is not these things in and of
themselves that create an unhappy life — it is the*
internal mental addiction or desire for them *that
minute-by-minute keeps one from enjoying life.
Since the nature of the world is such that we win
some and lose some, an addicted person has no
chance of living a happy, loving, peaceful,
conscious, wise, and effective life ....*

*... If you are not enjoying every here and now
moment in your life, it is because your addictions
(otherwise known as desires, attachments, demands,
expectations, emotional programming, models of
how life should treat you) are making you dwell in
the dead past or the imagined future. They are
keeping you from being here now. All there is in
your life is the eternal now moment — and your
experience of this moment is created by the
programming in your head ....*

The Present

*Lack of Life - Vision
or Posession Life - Vision*

*Your mind creates your universe. Your expecta-
tions, demands, hopes, fears, addictions,
motivations, past experience, your language system,
your individual accumulation of ideas, theories, and
intellectual stuff, your emotions, the structure and
functioning of your nervous system and the
feedback from your entire body all interact in a
complex way to produce your perceptions — the
"picture" you create from the energies you receive
through your various senses from people and things
around you ...*

*Avoid Dealings With The World Will mirror
Your World Will mirror   either Your Posession
or Lack of An Accurate
Life - Vision*

*... The world thus tends to be your mirror. A
peaceful person lives in a peaceful world. An angry
person creates an angry world. A happy person
finds the world full of happy people — for even*

unhappy people experience temporary happiness
and joy when they are with a genuinely happy and
joyous person....

These words from the *Handbook To Higher Consciousness* made the happiness game clear for me, and I thank the author, Ken Keyes, Jr., for letting me share these thoughts with you. I realized that my friends and I were addicted. We were stuck in our belief systems that said that happiness came from *doing things* or *having things*. But it was one thing to understand the games we were playing. It was another to learn to stop playing them. After all, we had played those games so long that we felt they were part of us. The one game that seemed to dominate was the "I'll be happy when ..." game.

Many of us begin playing the "I'll be happy when ..." game before we go to grade school. We say "I'll be happy when I'm old enough to cross the street." When we are allowed to cross the street by ourselves, we say "I'll be happy when I can ride the bus to school." When we are in school, we say "I'll be happy when I graduate," then "I'll be happy when I get my own car," then "I'll be happy when I find a person to love," and so on. Eventually, we do find loving relationships, but are we happy then? No, we still are discontent and say we'll be happy if we land a good job. Then we say we'll be happy when we have plenty of money, a permanent loving relationship, and some security. Then when all this comes, we want more excitement in life, more travel, more friends. So, we travel and find more thrills. But we are still not "happy." Some people hope to be happier when they retire and have more time. When happiness still fails to come, they may look forward to dying to be happy in heaven. I have never been to heaven, but I imagine people there are not content being in the now. They're probably trying to get closer and closer to God thinking that would make them happier.

Let's stop for a minute and see where you are in this game. What did you promise yourself would make you happy ten years ago? Do you have it now? Are you satisfied or are you planning what you need ten years from now? Is it clear to you that happiness never comes to those who continually search for it? The truth is that it can be here and now.

Wouldn't you love to be able to convince teenagers that these are great years in their lives? They have youth, time, freedom from much responsibility, and friends. Who could ask for more? Teenagers, of course. And what is wrong with life at your age? The answer is: Nothing is wrong unless people make it so. Life can always be good now, but it loses some of its now value when your mind compares it with past thrills or future thrills. That process often starts around age five and never seems to end.

The only way to break the cycle of more, more, more is to change our belief system. But that is very difficult. Our whole life has been devoted to living up to our beliefs. To give them up would be to give up everything we have worked for, everything we have done. Or would it? Couldn't we simply acknowledge that we have come this far with our present beliefs but now wish to move on to something different?

THE TRYING GAME

Look around you and notice the people who are playing the "trying" game. Some are *trying* to lose weight. Others are trying to be more friendly. Others are trying to get a better education. But notice also that people who "try" never seem to succeed.

Most people try too hard. Whatever they are trying does not come naturally for them. Many people try to escape from what they are, but that is impossible. What must occur first is acceptance of who we are and what we are. For example, people can accept the fact that they are overweight and realize that they have chosen to be that. These people must not reject that state. They must adopt a feeling of total love and respect for themselves first. That is, "I'm OK *and* I think I'll lose some weight." Such an attitude does not cause a battle between mind and Self. The mind will not reject new Self (slim person) because new Self does not reject what is. Do you see?

You have struggles between your mind and your Self, and you have struggles with other people. In all these struggles, acting out of love cures the "trying" game. You do not have to "try" to make new friends if you act out of love. Similarly, you do not have to "try" to improve yourself if you act out of love of *Self.* You just do it.

A TOTAL PRE-GAME WARM UP

We have learned that there are two main steps to preparing for the happiness game: (1) learning to manage the mind by meditating (concentrating on what you are doing), and (2) stopping the games our minds play ("I'll be happy when ..." and "winning"). The following exercise outlines the steps to follow in your pre-game warm up:

1. Notice all the discomfort your mind causes you because of its skepticism, prejudices, evaluations, and limiting beliefs.
2. Commit yourself 100% to becoming a happy, self-confident, aware, and loving person.
3. Notice what attracts your attention naturally (e.g., music or beautiful scenery).
4. Whenever your mind begins sending you negative thoughts, stop what you are doing, close your eyes, breathe deeply several times, and focus on your naturally attractive setting. Notice details and become aware of the relaxed, happy state of being that results.
5. Experience the feeling of acceptance of "who you are" and "what you have" that results from meditating. That is what happiness feels like.

Warming Up

6. Notice your beliefs about success and winning. Notice further how brief the joy is that results from winning.
7. Choose a career and games that are fun to play and play them for fun. Notice how much time you are willing to devote to those games *when they are fun.* Notice also the increase in energy and the happiness that you feel in such situations.
8. Let personal growth come naturally. Practice all you will learn here, but don't *judge* yourself as you go along. You will have a chance to chart your progress.

Personal growth comes as naturally to people who get rid of their addictions as growth comes to a flower. You are not incomplete where you are in life. You are simply in the process of becoming the beautiful person you were always meant to be. Relax and let it happen.

SCORING THE GAME

Who is winning control over your life, your past beliefs and habits or your naturally happy Self? Can you relax and play the game of life without needing to win? Score yourself from 1 to 10 depending on how accurately you feel the following statements describe you — 1 means "not at all" and 10 means "perfectly."

How Well Do You Manage Your Mind Now?

Statement	Now	After 6 Months	After 1 Year
1. I am committed to being happy *now*, not when a change occurs in my life.	5		
2. I have control over my thoughts.	1		
3. I am willing to give up my limiting beliefs.	5		
4. I am not addicted to winning.	1		
5. I have learned to control my thoughts by concentrating on naturally attractive things (meditating).	2		
6. I can see clearly the beliefs that are getting in my way of experiencing happiness.	2		
7. I am growing naturally without struggling or judging myself.	1		
8. I accept responsibility for my feelings.	8		
9. Happiness is a priority in my life.	8		
10. I create my own experience.	5		
Total Score			

Starting Date _____

Notice there is no chart to compare yourself with others. There are no *bad* scores, only scores that reveal a person's progress in expressing his or her potential. Notice, though, whether you wanted to score well. Notice too how you feel about your score. Did you want to *win* by scoring well? What was your "voice" saying as you played the game? Was it critical of you? Of the questions? Notice the dialogue between you and your mind and remember that you can shut it off. Happiness is the ability to appreciate fully what you are doing now. That means that every moment of every day gives you a chance to review your search for happiness, including this moment. Enjoy what you are doing. That is the key.

Chapter 4

Getting the Field Ready for Play

*B*efore playing the happiness game, the field of play must be cleared of all rocks that get in the way of your enjoyment — particularly rocks such as fear, worry, and guilt. These obstacles are hard to be rid of because our minds are attached to them. But the feelings are natural and, fortunately, they are manageable.

REMOVING THE FEAR OBSTACLE

One emotion that keeps us from living life fully is fear. It keeps us from trying new experiences, forming new friendships, joining new groups, and acting out our true feelings.

When I was in the eighth grade, I thought I would enjoy playing football. But since I weighed only 85 pounds, I was afraid of being hurt. The equipment was rather primitive in those days — no face masks, cardboard shoulder pads, and soft leather helmets. Therefore, I asked myself a question that has served me well through the years, "What is the worst thing that can happen to me?" I figured that the worst that would happen was breaking an arm, leg, or nose. Then I asked myself "Could I live with that?" The answer was a definite yes, so I played football. And I did not get hurt.

I have had many other fears in my lifetime. I was afraid to ask out certain girls, afraid to take my doctoral exams, afraid to teach graduate courses, afraid to write a book, afraid to ski, and afraid to invest in an expensive home. In each instance, I have asked the same question, "What is the worst that can happen?" Then I asked, "Can I live with that?" If the answer is *yes,* I tried it, and then I made sure the worst never happened.

One way to conquer fear, therefore, is to ask yourself what is the worst thing that can happen, think it through, and see if you can accept it. If so, go ahead. If not, explore why not and see if you are not exaggerating the dangers or the consequences.

If, in spite of all your preparation, the worst happens, accept that fact and move on. Do not use one case as an example for yourself that you are a failure. To fail at something does not make a person a failure. A failure is someone who has failed and as a consequence stops trying. A winner is someone who has failed and kept trying until he or she succeeded.

Another helpful technique for overcoming fear is to ask "How important is this thing to me personally?" If you were to fail to make the team, to get the date, or to win the game, how would *you* feel? Too often people worry about how *others* would feel. If I do not make the team, my friends will laugh at me. If I ask her out, I will be embarrassed if she says "no" because she will laugh at me. The worst thing in life is *not* to look foolish or to have people laugh at you. *The worst thing in life is to be afraid to look foolish and have others laugh at you.* To test the real significance of a fearful event, look inward. If *you* are not seriously affected by the outcome, try it knowing you will not feel bad if you fail. You would be surprised how others leave you alone when they know you cannot be embarrassed about having tried and not succeeded.

By the way, others cannot make you embarrassed. They can laugh and tease and point, but only *you* can make yourself embarrassed. The best way to avoid ridicule is to laugh first and loudest at your mistakes. You can have no fear of being embarrassed by others when you approach each challenge with a sense of humor and having full knowledge that you might not succeed. Life will go on anyhow; that is for sure.

PRACTICE REDUCES FEAR

There's another way of overcoming fear, too. Stop and think what is it that you are *not* afraid of? Most people are not afraid of doing things that are quite familiar. So another key to conquering fear is practicing until you are so comfortable doing something that you have no fear.

I have been afraid to sing in front of others, to ride a bike, to try exotic foods, to lecture in front of large groups, and to write books. The initial drive to overcome most of these fears was my overriding desire to earn a living and have fun. To earn a living, I learned to lecture in front of large groups (I teach sections of 500 students) and to write books (this is my third). I learned to lecture by practicing alone in my room. When I felt confident I knew the material well, I would face the audience *knowing* I could do it. I also practiced writing. Like most people my age, I was not taught the fundamentals of writing in school; consequently, writing did not come easily. I had to practice, tear up my material, practice some more, get help, practice, get more help, and practice again. Soon I was able to write well enough to start a book. But I was still afraid of not finding a publisher and of people rejecting my ideas. But I tried. I sent material out to reviewers, I rewrote, and eventually I gained confidence. I still make many mistakes, but I am no longer afraid to try.

Sometimes a task may be so formidable that you're afraid even to try practicing. In that case, you must practice doing small parts of the whole task until fear of that part is conquered. Then you can move on to another part. For example, people who are afraid of snakes begin by standing several feet from a rubber snake. After some practice, they move within a few feet, and eventually can touch the rubber snake. The next step is to stand several feet from a small, real snake. Again, the person moves closer at his own pace until the snake can be touched and held.

What are your fears? What steps could be made to break that fear down into manageable units? List those steps and practice them one by one, maybe just in your mind. If you fear water, for example, you could go to the beach, then stand in the water, then splash in the water, then splash in a pool, then put your head under the water while standing in a shallow place, then lie down in the water, practice kicking your feet, then move your arms, next float with a life vest or "wings," then *swim*. This process may take several years, but the end is worth it. After you practice conquering one fear, you will gain the courage to try another. Eventually you will find yourself taking on new challenges just for the thrill of testing yourself, and winning the game with yourself. The ultimate goal is to not play the fear game at all!

WARM-UP EXERCISES FOR OVERCOMING FEAR

Let's try practicing all these procedures for conquering fear:

1. Commit yourself 100% to trying new things.
2. Ask yourself, "What is the worst thing that can happen to me if I do it?" If you can handle the worst thing, then go for it knowing you can't lose. If you can't handle the worst thing, consider alternative solutions until you can.
3. Practice doing small parts of what you fear and keep doing more until you can do it all. With practice, the behavior will become automatic.
4. Look at the beliefs behind your fears. Just be aware of the limits that you impose on yourself with your beliefs.

REMOVING THE WORRY OBSTACLE

Montaigne wrote hundreds of years ago, "My life has been full of terrible misfortunes most of which never happened." He was particularly worried about his health. Have you ever seen people more worried about health than today? The papers are full of stories about potential health hazards. Everything either causes cancer or has cholesterol.

But what good is worrying? Will worry cure cancer? Will it make food healthier? Obviously, there is *no* benefit to worry. Worry kills the present moment by letting the mind dream up a horrible future.

Recently, I attended a conference at a lovely resort in Rhode Island. Several colleagues and I were standing around the bar talking when one of the men interjected that he was worried about his garden.

He had left for the conference without watering his plants and he was worried they might die. I asked him, "What will happen to the plants if you stop worrying?" He said, "They might die." "And what will happen if you do worry?" "They might die." This man was failing to fully enjoy his colleagues and the beautiful location by worrying about his garden. He felt that if he did not worry about things, he would not be motivated to take care of them. Good point, right? But does worrying water the garden? No, planning does.

Do not worry about the garden; set up a plan for watering it. If you can do something now, do it. If you can do something in the future, plan for it. That is the rule for getting things done.

REMOVING THE "BLAMING OTHERS" OBSTACLE

One of the most destructive attitudes is the one that says, "I am what I am because of some thing, some person, or some event, outside of myself." If people can blame people and events for their feelings and behavior, then they can justify not being responsible, not being happy, and not being alive to the world. But only one person has absolute control over your feelings — you. No one can "make" you happy or enthused.

On the other hand, you can't "make" others happy either. You can help create the environment that allows them to make themselves happy. Similarly, others can help create an environment that frees you to make yourself happy. But the person who is responsible for any feeling is the person who experiences that feeling — no one else.

Notice how messed up the world is because people don't accept responsibility for their own behavior. You have heard people say:

"This weather depresses me."
"This traffic makes me angry."
"School is driving me crazy."

"This movie makes me sad."

"My boss drives me crazy."

I could go on forever listing the reasons people give for their feelings and behavior. And maybe you have agreed with them in the past. But can you see the error in this thinking?

Weather is like it is, and some people are happy and others are sad. The weather did not make them that way. Similarly, school, movies, society, parents, and other outside influences are like they are. As a consequence, some people *make themselves* happy or sad, excited or depressed, responsible or not responsible, and so forth. You are the cause of your behavior and others are the cause of their behavior.

Let me give you an example. Because of some financial setbacks, my friend Joan had to go to work. She had graduated from college and had reared three children. Her work experience was limited to some part-time typing. Joan accepted a full-time job at her local high school doing some typing. She was miserable. She said, "This job *makes me* sad. The people *make me* upset. Everyone *puts me down* and this *hurts my* ego. The working conditions *make me* even more depressed. The lighting *gives me* a headache and the kids *drive me* crazy." Janet, who works in the same office, loves the work and the people. She says it *makes her* happy to work there and the people *make her* feel important and worthwhile.

The job at the high school is what it is. One person allows herself to be depressed, upset, and put down. Another allows herself to feel happy and worthwhile. It is not the job that creates peoples' reactions. *They do it themselves!* To get more enjoyment out of life, you only have to assume responsibility for your own feelings. You can *choose* your feelings, so why not choose happiness and self-satisfaction?

Blaming others is a habit. Taking responsibility can become a habit too. But it takes practice. This kind of practice is hard because it is difficult to blame ourselves for what we do. Our belief system resists the fact that we are responsible for our own feelings. Acknowledge that fact, and you will realize that the happiness battle is not as tough as you thought.

Before you read the next section, it is important to pause and write two very short lists. In one list, I want you to write 4-6 sentences describing yourself. In the other list, I want you to write 4-6 sentences describing the person you are most fond of (your spouse, a friend, your child). If you cannot make the lists, do them mentally and keep them in mind.

REMOVING THE STEREOTYPING OBSTACLE

After reading the literature and participating in human potential programs, I have concluded that one of the most destructive games in life is the "stereotyping" game. We all play this game and it is keeping us chained to the past.

We often use stereotypes when we describe ourselves. Here are some stereotypic phrases that prevent progress toward liberation of body, mind, and spirit:

"I am a nice person."
"I am a good worker."
"I am very generous."

You may feel that such statements are positive. After all isn't it good to be "nice," "a good worker," and "generous." The answer is yes and no. Sometimes it is good, but often it is terribly limiting.

For example, "I am a man" is a fact, not a belief. But stereotyping myself as a man *can* be limiting. Many people feel that *a man* would rarely cry. *A man* is strong, brave, and aggressive. *A man* does not love other men. And so on.

Much of today's domestic tension grows out of the "I am a man" and "I am a woman" game. Many women feel tied down by "women's work" and resent the attitude that women are "weak" and submissive. The women's liberation movement is a major attempt to stop stereotyping women. The movement is helping women as a whole, but individual women still tend to stereotype themselves.

Playing the "I am nice" game is just as destructive as the "I am a man/woman" game. *"Nice people* don't _____. (You fill in the blanks.) Nice people do not progress because progress sometimes involves doing things "nice" people do not *believe* are nice — things like being competitive, being assertive, and being outspoken. Isn't it better to be "nice"? No! Not if it means giving up your vitality and it often does.

Men are victims of the stereotyping syndrome. What is wrong with being stereotyped as brave, strong, responsible, and liberated? What *is* wrong is that these are tough images to live up to. How I long sometimes to show my weakness and ask for support. I am not always strong, and I don't always want to be responsible. Yet I feel that I must play the man game so I am not liberated either. I must not cry, at least in public. I must drink beer, act tough, and generally "be a man."

Where is the liberation movement for men? There is a "liberated male" movement, but the fact is that most men do not feel they need one. Some men enjoy playing the role of man and they like the idea that people think they are strong and brave and all that. But the truth is that they are just people. And people are vulnerable, people have weaknesses, and people need help. We are all oppressed and we all have limiting roles assigned to us. We all need help to find a more fulfilling role, a richer life, and a more liberated mind, body and spirit.

HOW YOU STEREOTYPE YOURSELF

Now go back to the sentences you used to describe yourself. Look through the sentences and see how each description imposes a limiting role on yourself. For example, if you said, "I am happy" you may think that is beneficial, but it may actually limit you. A "happy" person may avoid many potentially disrupting circumstances that could affect happiness. In short, a happy person might do *anything* to maintain that happiness, including living a restricted life. No person always feels happy. If you feel you should always feel happy you will be miserable when you're not. Remember, the happiness game is a game — sometimes you win and sometimes you lose. Losing is not bad; it just is. But, almost all stereotypes of Self are limiting. The only non-limiting one is "I am."

HOW YOU STEREOTYPE OTHERS

Another destructive game in life is stereotyping others. We all play that game too, and it tends to keep others chained to *their* part. We all need to escape from stereotypes. We must all do our part to help. We need human liberation — liberation from all those stereotypes, roles, and behavior we place on each other.

Let's explore a few such roles we impose:

> "You are a woman."
> "You are my son/daughter."
> "You are beautiful."
> "You are helpful."
> "You are brave."

Again, these statements seem harmles, and perhaps even supportive. Is it not supportive to tell someone that he or she is beautiful, helpful, or brave? The answer is yes and no. It is as damaging to expect someone to act like a woman or a daughter as it is to play that role. Men sometimes expect women to be relatively weak, or dependent. How destructive that is of a full and mutually supportive relationship. Similarly, a woman can destroy a man by expecting him to be brave and strong. All of the concepts we discussed before apply here. It is very limiting to play any role, *and* it is very limiting to expect any role from others.

Without stereotypes we just are. We have no defenses, we have no past or future. Without stereotypes we must live in the now. We are free to enjoy *what is* without comparing it to what was or what could be. We are free to enjoy who we are with without wanting to be different. This freedom allows people to become everything we like them to be. We cannot *force* them to change, but by letting them go, we *allow* them to change. All of us want to please others, but we also want to defend our "old self." By letting people get rid of "old self," we free them to be "new self." And "new self" is very likely to be what we are looking for it we do not impose any stereotypes.

Suppose you tell your child how capable he or she is and how proud that makes you. Being eager to please, your child will try hard to seem capable. But some things will come along that he or she will not be able to do well, at least initially. Rather than appear awkward, the child is likely to not try at all. How disappointing that can be both to the child and the parent.

"I wish John would play golf with me," a parent said. But John did not know how to play golf and was embarrassed to play in front of his father. His father thought his son was athletic and "a natural" at all sports. To live up to that image, his son played only those sports he excelled in. How limiting. How unfair to both.

HOW YOU STEREOTYPE PEOPLE YOU CARE ABOUT

Now go back over that list you made describing a person you are fond of. What expectations do you raise by those descriptions? What limits do your expectations place on that person? Are you willing to free that person to be what he or she is? Or would you rather have some control?

When you have control, you have control over a puppet, an unreal plaything. When you have a relationship, you get cooperation but lose control. Both of you are free to grow and be happy and that is exciting. But freedom is frightening. Nobody knows where it leads; so we want limits. But limits keep us and others from playing the happiness game.

REMOVING THE EVALUATION OBSTACLE

Another destructive game in life is the "evaluation" game. Again, it's a game we all play and it keeps us from getting full enjoyment out of life. Pause here for a moment and make a list of things that you feel are "good." This list should be rather long. When you are finished, write another list of things you feel are "bad." A typical "good" list might include:

Sunny, warm weather
Vacations
Close friends
Freedom
Knowledge
Humor
Truth
Love
Courage
Happiness

Because most of us would agree these things are good, we tend to classify everything in these areas as "good" and everything counter to these areas "bad." If sunny, warm weather is "good" then cold, rainy weather becomes "bad." If "truth" is "good," then telling people what we think is good as long as it is true. For example, in the name of truth, we might tell someone he looks fat or funny or silly. If "education" is good, we will attend classes and read books we do not enjoy.

The problem is obvious. Most of us are doing things because we feel they are "good." But as a consequence we end up doing things that we really do not enjoy. The problem is that we evaluate things and cling to those evaluations.

The remedy is to stop evaluating. It is *not* always "good" to be brave, strong, responsible or capable. It is *not* always "bad" to be weak, to be awkward, or to be irresponsible. Notice how we can ruin our lives by playing the "good" and "bad" game. What we can strive for is finding the "OK" in everything we see or hear or do. Then we can reach for the ultimate in happiness: Letting what is *be* without finding any need to make it good or bad.

What benefit do we derive from such judgments? If things are good, we can enjoy them without having to say they are good. If things are not so good, we can manage them if we do not make them bad or worse yet by our judgments.

REVIEWING OUR GOOD-BAD LIST

Look over your list of bads. What makes such things bad? Are they part of life? Will making them bad make us happier? Will making them bad make others happier? Let's look at some examples of what some people call bad:

Selfishness
Moodiness
Fear
Losing
Worry
Hate
Deceit
Injustice

We need not dwell on the problems caused by making these

things bad. Life is full of injustice, hatred and lies. To make them bad is to make much of life bad. Does that mean we should advocate such things? Obviously not. The fact is that we should try to minimize the negatives in our lives.

Why let "bad" thoughts linger in your mind? Burn those lists you made. Get rid of those past prejudices and judgments. How are things now? Are you tempted to say "good" or "bad?" Things now *are* — period. Don't make them bad. Take notice of them, notice the feelings they cause in you, notice that you can control those feelings by thinking of something else, and notice that you do not have to think "bad" — "good."

REMOVING THE ILLNESS OBSTACLE

It is widely believed that many illnesses (70-80%) are psychosomatic. That is, the mind plays tricks with the body and breaks down its natural resistance to disease. This is usually a cooperative effort. Belief systems force people to work hard, get tense, and seek more. People get tired and need a break. The mind responds by breaking down resistance to disease, and people get sick and are forced to relax.

No doubt you have noticed that some people get sick often and others never get sick. Did it ever occur to you that sick people may have *chosen* to be sick and well people may have *chosen* to be healthy? At first this hypothesis may seem ridiculous — why would anyone *choose* to be sick? But some people get more out of being sick than being well.

Margaret McInnes was an only child. She was the center of the family's attention. When Margaret was 5, her mother became pregnant again and had Jimmy Junior. Jimmy was a bright, healthy child and immediately captured the attention of the family. One day Margaret became ill with the flu. The whole family turned to Margaret

Getting the Field Ready for Play

and gave her meals in bed, read to her, and generally administered to her needs. She was out of school for four days and again received lots of special attention.

Margaret is 28 now. She is sickness prone. Margaret seems to catch every virus that passes through town. Jim, her little brother, is almost never ill. People feel sorry for Margaret and wonder how there could be such a variance in health in one family. Can you think of an explanation for Margaret's perpetual illnesses other than a "weak defense system?" Could it be that Margaret uses sickness to get sympathy and attention? We will never know why Margaret was often ill, but after going through a personal growth program her illnesses vanished! Now at 29, Margaret is confident she can live a healthy and happy life. And no doubt she will.

Chances are that Margaret was one of the vast majority of sick people who *chose* to be ill. Does this mean that they are not really ill? No, they are really ill. But the illness was not caused by some external virus alone; it was caused partially by their willingness to let a virus make them ill. Sounds incredible, doesn't it? But it makes more sense when you see how effective illness is in getting attention, excusing poor work, winning sympathy, and generally serving as a way to gain control over others.

So what is the secret of health? One answer is to become responsible for your commitments. A president who is committed to see a head of state on Monday, to make a major TV address on Tuesday, and to sign or veto a major piece of legislation on Wednesday has little time for sickness. He or she has too many commitments to keep. The drive to keep those commitments helps generate the antibodies to fight off minor illnesses.

But remember that many illnesses are *not* psychosomatic. People do break legs and catch infections. Therefore you cannot say that all people *choose* illness. But you can say with confidence that *most illness* is aided by the ill people themselves, along with germs or allergens or some other external source. Through a lack of willpower

THE HAPPINESS GAME

67

and commitment, these people allow themselves not only to get sick, but to stay sick for days, weeks or even years.

Of course, another way people choose not to be healthy is by eating junk foods, smoking cigarettes, avoiding exercise, getting fat, and generally abusing their bodies. Often these choices are more conscious than the choice to be sick.

To choose health, you must not only make and keep commitments to others, you must make and keep commitments to Self. This means feeding yourself proper foods, getting exercise, and keeping yourself fit. This is an active commitment to health. Health and happiness are so closely related that most personal growth programs, including the happiness game, often include physical exercise as part of the training.

No matter what we do, there will be periods when illness strikes. If we do not allow our beliefs to make illness bad, we have a great opportunity to spend some time relaxing. Let's explore this further below.

SICKNESS IS NATURE'S WAY OF SAYING "SLOW DOWN"

Ron Langston was working at a furious pace. He had reports to complete and final arrangements to make before leaving on a business trip. The day before he was to leave, Ron caught the Russian flu.

Ron was in bed for four days. He missed his trip and his assistant finished the report. The first day Ron felt very weak — he couldn't move out of bed and had aches and pains throughout his body. A dull headache kept him from doing much thinking. The second day Ron still felt weak, but most of the aches and pains were gone. Ron enjoyed his stay in bed and relaxed, read the paper, and finished a novel he had started weeks before. On the third day, Ron accepted several calls from his friends and enjoyed talking with his children and sharing the day with them. By the fourth day, Ron felt good enough to go to work but decided to rest at home instead. He felt the tensions of work might be too much too soon.

As he rested in bed, Ron had several good ideas about ways to reorganize his job. He saw clearly the answers to problems that had bothered him for weeks. He also had a new perspective on family versus work. In short, Ron returned to work a new man. He took on fewer responsibilities and got more done on the projects he accepted. He also spent more time at home.

Sickness is nature's way of saying, "Slow down." It gives us time to think and get a new perspective on life. Sickness is a real opportunity to relieve the pressures of work, an opportunity to relax and renew old friendships, and an opportunity to reflect on our lives and what is really important in them. Rather than curse sickness for coming at a busy time, we should take advantage of the opportunity to be less busy and make plans to get better control over our lives.

There is much to be said about never being sick. But if you are never ill, you are missing an opportunity to change your life. So when sickness strikes your home, be ready to use it to your advantage!

LAUGH THERAPY

Laughter is a powerful medicine. No one knows that better than Norman Cousins. Doctors told him he had a case of degenerative connective tissues of the spine. Nothing the doctors did seemed to help much. He was fed up with aspirin and other pain killing drugs. He wanted a cure.

Cousins *believed in* the concepts of the self development literature. He knew that negative emotions caused a chemical reaction in the body that could cause physical harm. He felt it must also be true that positive emotions could work wonders. So Cousins designed his own laugh therapy.

THE HAPPINESS GAME

He had nurses read him humorous writings and he watched funny movies. Cousins found that a good belly laugh acted as an anesthetic giving him a couple of hours free of pain. As the pain returned, more laughter turned it off.

Laughter and massive intake of vitamin C were his only medicines. Both did their job marvelously and Cousins is now back at work. Since Cousins reported his experiences in the *New England Journal of Medicine,* and his bestselling book *Anatomy Of An Illness As Perceived By The Patient,* he has received many letters from people with similar experiences. They shared their experiences of negative emotions which destroy mind, body and spirit, and positive emotions which fortify mind, body and spirit.

Positive emotions include a sense of humor. And, it's important that the first source of humor be yourself. You cannot help but laugh at the silly games you play if you back off and watch yourself objectively. Practice smiling at yourself and others. Build that smile into a lively sense of humor. Let yourself go and laugh out loud. Laugh long and laugh hard whenever you get a chance. And if you have few such chances, make time to put more laughter into your life.

WITHOUT OBSTACLES, LIFE IS AN ADVENTURE

Living in the now can become so enjoyable that people become afraid to move on and try new things. *That fear will probably always be there.* There is no way to make life an adventure if you insist on it being under your control. The fun of adventure is in *not knowing* and going for it anyway. And making it all right no matter what happens.

When you control the flow of events in your life, the events are always controlled. There is no spontaneity, no thrill of discovery, no going beyond. You have to take a risk to be in the game; there is no hiding in the bleachers. There is no alternative. Being in the game means going for it whether or not you are fully prepared because you never know for sure what will happen. Here are the procedures for getting those doubts and fears and worries out of your way:

1. Commit yourself 100% to get as much out of life as you can. That is 100%, not 99%.

2. Keep your agreements to yourself and others always. That builds self-trust, self-confidence and the trust and confidence of others.

3. Ask yourself, "What is the worst thing that can happen to me if I go for it?" Can you handle that? If you can't, commit yourself 100% and then go for it anyway. Take the risk and see what happens.

5. Live moment to moment to moment when you take the risk. Don't anticipate! Wait and see what happens. Experience the thrill of being in the game and let the events come as they may. Enjoy the adventure. *There is no right path on adventure.*

6. If you begin to worry, notice that and include it as part of the game for now. Notice that worry sometimes occurs in life and keep going moment by moment. Worry can be part of the adventure. Do you think that people who parachute from planes aren't worried? Are you kidding? But they go for it anyway — and what an experience! Get involved 100% and you won't have time for worry.

7. Don't evaluate the events that occur when you go for it. Give up the "good-bad" game for a while. Let the game go on and you will see that what seemed an insurmountable obstacle will disappear.

8. Now that you are in your adventure, notice how stereotypes have been limiting you and drop the ones you are still holding. You are afraid and that is good because you are going for it anyway and fear is part of the game. Men and women take risks, both worry about how they look to others, and both, deep down

inside, are little boys and girls playing grown up. So? Playing grown up is much easier than being one, isn't it? Give up the stereotype that adults *are* adults and must act that way.

9. Finally, notice that when you finally decide to go for it, when experiencing the thrill of taking the risk, when you have a clear purpose in life — sickness fades away. If sickness comes, take it as a signal from your body that either (1) it is worn out from being involved 100% (doubtful) or (2) it is testing your determination to go on. If you are truly incapacitated, take the time to reaffirm your commitments and agreements. Your sickness will be over when you are ready to go 100% again.

SCORING THE GAME

How well have you learned to handle the negative events in your life? Are you relatively free from fear, doubt, and self-destroying behavior? Score yourself from 1 to 10 depending on how accurately you feel the following statements describe you — 1 means "not at all" and 10 means "perfectly."

WHAT OBSTACLES REMAIN IN YOUR LIFE?

Statements	Now	After 6 Months	After 1 Year
1. I take responsibility for my life.	————	————	————
2. When I have fear in my life, I "go for it" anyway.	————	————	————
3. I rarely worry.	————	————	————
4. I have not stereotyped myself.	————	————	————
5. Life is an adventure and I've learned to take what comes.	————	————	————
6. I am rarely ill.	————	————	————
7. I laugh a lot.	————	————	————
8. I am willing to take risks.	————	————	————
9. I do not stereotype others.	————	————	————
10. I do not judge everything as "good" or "bad."	————	————	————
Total Scores	————	————	————

Starting Date _____

Chapter 5

Developing Happiness Skills through Practice

*H*ave you ever tried to teach someone a game such as tennis? Many beginners constantly talk as they learn. The chatter goes something like this, "I know I'll never learn this, I'm not the athletic type. See that, I missed again; boy, am I bad. This isn't fun, I just don't get it." That chatter is their "voice" reflecting their beliefs. Some beginners never break through those limiting beliefs; others do. The key to success is accepting the fact that no one is good at something without practicing. Beginners are not "bad" players; they are merely beginners.

We have said that part of happiness is the ability to appreciate fully who we are now. That does not mean we are stuck where we are. We can be all we hope to be. All it takes is lots of practice and the self-confidence to go on. But first we need self-confidence. Self-confidence comes from affirming who we are now and seeing all the potential we now have. A beginning tennis player and a beginning happiness player have much in common. Both are likely to feel awkward at first. Both will have to conquer negative beliefs about themselves as told to them by their "voices." Both have the potential for becoming better players. All they need is practice. This chapter will discuss techniques for practicing happiness skills.

THE VALUE OF PRACTICE

People tend to decide very early in life what they are and are not good at. They say things such as "I'm not good at spelling" or "I'm not athletic" or "I'm not good at math" or "I'm shy." These people have stereotyped themselves as failures. It only takes one thing to learn to spell — practice. Similarly, to learn math takes practice, to learn athletics takes practice and to learn to be outgoing takes practice.

Most people understand the value of practice, but don't realize how widely applicable practice can be. Everyone learns how to walk, talk, swim, ride, whistle, read and write by practicing. Yet it often never occurs to people that they can also learn to be happy, outgoing, athletic, and enthusiastic by practicing these traits.

Some people seem naturally friendly and others wonder how they got that way. The answer — by practicing. Have you ever noticed how beauty queens radiate friendliness? You immediately warm up to them because they always seem to be smiling. But smiling is not easy to do. Try smiling for hours, as beauty contestants do, and you will see how tired it makes your face muscles. At first it seems artificial, but if you practice long and hard, smiling becomes easy and everyone will say you have a "natural" smile.

No matter what we do, we do it after much practice. For example, there is no such things as a shy person; there are only people who think they are shy.

OVERCOMING SHYNESS

The one personality disorder that dominates all others in its ability to interfere with the happiness game is shyness. All people have experienced periods of shyness in their lives; times when they have felt nervous about approaching a new group. You know how it feels. Multiply by ten the nervousness and hesitation a normal person feels in social situations, and you have some idea what it is like to be very shy. The symptoms are loneliness, self-doubt, and self-pity. The physiological signs include excessive perspiration, irregular breathing, and a pounding heart whenever the person is faced with social interaction. But it is easy to overcome shyness. All it takes is practice.

Joey had a very strict father. Whenever Joey would cry, his father would shout, "Sit down and shut up." Periodically Joey's father would hit him and send him to his room if Joey made too much noise. Joey learned very early that to avoid being yelled at he would have to be quiet. And he became good at being quiet — by practicing. Now Joey is 21 and will soon graduate from college. Joey says he *is* shy and he has tremendous difficulty speaking in front of others. He has trouble making friends and does not enjoy dancing, singing, or being with people in general. You see, Joey has practiced all of his life avoiding people and now he seems like a "naturally" shy person.

To become a more outgoing person, Joey has to practice. It will not be easy. Old habits have to be changed, and new approaches practiced. Like a beginning piano player, Joey will make mistakes. He will be embarrassed and want to stop. The process will go slowly and painfully, but the rewards will be great.

THE HAPPINESS GAME

EXERCISES FOR OVERCOMING SHYNESS

The techniques for overcoming shyness are too complex to detail in this book, but here are some techniques you can try. If these aren't helpful, investigate shyness courses offered in your community.

1. Commit yourself 100% to becoming outgoing and self-confident.

2. Read books about shyness to learn how successful the new techniques are.

3. Practice being more open by saying "Hi!" and smiling at people you meet for 10 minutes a day. Gradually work up to all day.

4. Assume the role of an outgoing person by changing how you dress, how you walk, and how you talk. Think through social situations in your mind and see yourself as being funny, warm, and outgoing.

5. Practice playing the role of an outgoing person with strangers (such as the clerks at local retail stores).

6. Practice playing an outgoing role with your family. If you feel resistance to the new you, practice overcoming that resistance in your mind first, and then do it again with family members.

7. Practice your new role with friends and co-workers.

8. Explore other limiting beliefs about yourself now that you are learning to talk with people. Notice that almost *everyone* has such beliefs, so you are not alone.

9. Go to a shyness clinic for help if you get stuck in your progress, but seek self-reliance as soon as you can.

10. Keep reading this book to learn more happiness skills. The better you get at other skills, the easier it becomes to overcome shyness.

Developing Happiness Skills through Practice

NEGATIVE PRACTICING

Most of us have practiced all of our lives to be what we are. Now we have a strong commitment to that. We have programmed our minds, through practice and repetition, to believe certain things of ourselves. Some of the negative programming looks like this:

"Smoke makes me sick."

"Not eating gives me a headache."

"I am clumsy."

"I am not a good listener."

"I am poor in athletics."

"I never have been able to get along with strangers."

"I can't dance."

Take a minute here and think of your own negative programming. What do you believe about yourself? That you cannot be happy because _____? That you cannot enjoy life fully because of your handicap which keeps you from _____? That you are not _____?

Examine *all* of your beliefs about what is "right" and "wrong". Let go of the hates and prejudices and behavior that you have practiced so long. Notice again that voice in your head telling you that you *have* to love certain people and *ought* to visit them. In fact, explore all of the "oughts" and "shoulds" and "have tos." Stop for a minute and go through your beliefs. Let me get you started.

What do you believe about the kinds of food you like?

What do you believe love is?

What do you believe a happy person should be like?

What do you believe about God?

What do you believe you can do well?

What do you believe about success?

What do you believe about winning?

What do you believe you do poorly?

What do you believe about your friends?

What do you believe about the nature of man?

What do you believe about rich people versus poor people?

If you stop and think about each of these questions, you will become more aware of your beliefs. Your mind will tell you they are correct — after all, you have practiced believing them for years. "Being right" is very important to some people. Some people would rather be "right" in their beliefs about people than accept them for what they really are.

For example, some people feel very strongly that a person who loves someone could never cheat on that person, lie, or do other mean things. If a person does cheat, they believe that is "proof" that the person does not love them. To be "right" about that, they will leave a loving relationship and practice hating for life.

All other lifelong beliefs can get in the way of progress toward happiness. They can all lead to the "I'm right" game and playing the "I'm right" game keeps people from playing other, more fun games.

BELIEF IN WHAT IS RIGHT

Let's explore ideas about beliefs a little further. If you believe that you won't like certain foods, your belief often hinders your experiencing of that food. The new food may actually be a delightful experience. If you believe that certain kinds of behavior are "wrong" or "inappropriate," those beliefs can prevent your trying new behaviors. For example, you may believe that singing in public is inappropriate. But that belief could keep you from enjoying singing out even when the mood does catch you.

Perhaps the most destructive belief of all is the belief that life is not meant for happiness and self fulfillment. This belief can hold people back from experiencing life. Some people believe that self development programs teach selfishness, are "rip-offs," or are a "waste of time." These beliefs get in their way of experiencing books such as this or other self development programs. But life is great and self development programs can do much to make life more joyful and more productive — you should experience it for yourself so you *know*.

Now what is your voice telling you? Notice it. Be aware of the constant evaluation it is making of what you read.

SUBSTITUTING EXPERIENCE AND AWARENESS FOR BELIEFS

If you try, you will discover a variety of little ways that you are letting your beliefs stop you from fully enjoying yourself everyday. Each time that happens, ask yourself if it is worth holding on to that belief. If it gets in your way, say "no" to that belief and say it with conviction and force. If at first you do not succeed, try it again next time that belief gets in your way of fun.

For example, every time your belief system keeps you from dancing or singing or playing a sport or participating in a group activity, notice it; notice also how it gets in your way of fun, and try again to reject it. The more you notice how your beliefs are keeping you from joyful living, the more likely you are to reject them.

Then you must practice your new behavior over and over until it too seems "right" to you. Happiness can be a habit too. If you have to choose between happiness and restrictive old patterns of behavior, why choose the latter? But you have to be determined about this. You must put yourself into situations where old beliefs keep you from doing fun things that you know you would enjoy doing. Then you must get really angry at yourself. Then yell at yourself and demand that you grow. Get serious about it! You can beat your old beliefs and gain control of your life if you really are sincere and if you practice.

MENTAL PRACTICING

We learned with shyness that not all practicing has to be physical. You can practice many things mentally. Many of the best golfers practice strokes in their heads. Similarly, gymnasts, basketball players, tennis players, and other athletes practice improving their skills in their head. The idea is to program the mind to respond correctly by habit. The mind controls the body, but the body can train the mind.

Practicing positive mental thoughts is very important in the happiness game. "I am capable," "I am happy," and "I am in charge," are examples of statements that should be programmed into your mind. When these thoughts are fed to your mind, your mind will begin demanding that you live up to your thoughts. It will demand that you stop downgrading yourself; be more optimistic, be more friendly, be more outgoing; and it will demand that you smile and be happy. The idea is to develop a positive self image and clear goals and then let the mind take over.

ACTING IS PRACTICING

Sometimes it is difficult to cast off the old you, the one who has all those hang-ups, doubts, fears, and hesitations. In that case, it is helpful to act the part of a different person. You become an actor and play the game of life as someone else.

If you want to be friendlier, play the part of a friendlier person. You can also act the role of a confident person; a relaxed person; a helpful, kind, and loving person; and a happy, and successful person. But acting takes practice, too. Eventually, after much practice, the part becomes second nature and you become the person you are playing.

You are playing a role now, one you have worked on for years. If it is not a particularly attractive role, get rid of it and assume a new one. Assume several new ones until you find one that results in a happier, more contented, more confident, more relaxed, and more comfortable you.

All this acting is great fun. Your "part" can go dancing and leave "you" behind. Your "part" has no past, only a future. Your new Self can try anything you would like, even knowing that "you" would never do such a thing. Soon the acting will be unnecessary. You will have tried new things and found them enjoyable. Yes, playing a new role in life is often better than living it with old Self. You can write your own script, change roles at will, and change the whole show if things go wrong.

It is not always easy to become comfortable with a new role. Your friends, co-workers, and family may create an environment where your old ways of doing things seem more appropriate. But every time you break through the temptation to revert, you will strengthen the new behavior and make it part of you. Furthermore, you will get so much enjoyment out of acting self-confident, happy, and self-assertive that you will keep up the practice until your mind demands you *be* that person. Finally you will be practicing a new total role — living in the *now*.

PRACTICE STROKING OTHERS

So far, we have been talking about ways of increasing our own happiness, but so much concentration on Self sounds like the human potential movement is one big ego trip. The fact is that human growth demands reaching out to others.

"Stroking" is a word out of transactional analysis (TA). Basically, *it means listening to, giving support to and generally being loving to others.* Few of us receive as much stroking as we would like. On the other hand, hardly anyone does as much stroking as they might. Stroking comes out of the feeling that "I'm OK, you're OK."

That is, I accept you as you are and as you are not. Please accept me the same way.

It is not difficult to give people "strokes." All it takes is a smile or a reassuring hug or some other sign of support. For example, a death in the family or a sudden illness sometimes causes people to lose focus. For them, being stroked involves someone just "being there" — not even talking or listening.

Even though that kind of stroking sounds easy, stroking does not come naturally to most people. It takes practice. You can begin by taking an hour each day and giving something to each person you meet. You might give them a smile, a compliment, or a kind word. Later, you can do this for a couple of hours a day and then one day a week. With enough practice, you will do it habitually, all the time. You will begin to radiate warmth, acceptance, and love.

Have you ever noticed how some people can light up a room with their presence? You feel relaxed and confident with them. They have an inner light that shines through the human mask most of us put on. They are able to stroke others with no obvious effort, and they almost never make fun of people. Notice that these people are not necessarily the best looking, most talented, or most intelligent people you know. They are merely the best at being themselves — open, honest and warm. They learned those skills and practice them daily.

Try playing the role of such a person for an hour a day. Increase to two hours, and so on. Stroking will give you a great deal of pleasure and provide you with a warm reception from others. After playing such a role for hours, you won't want to return to any role that involves being unsupportive, or unkind!

PRACTICE STROKING YOURSELF

Now that you have practiced stroking others, you are ready to tackle a more difficult assignment — stroking yourself. You should practice being at least as good and understanding with yourself as with others.

Developing Happiness Skills through Practice

84

But first you must learn (and that takes practice) to love yourself.

You have probably learned to be tolerant of others. For example, you can be patient, and loving. But can you be as patient with yourself? Only with practice. First you must recognize that it is easy to let others be as they are — warts and all. In theory it's just as easy to lighten up on yourself. But in practice it's much more difficult.

You can learn by using the same techniques you use to stroke others. Spend one hour a day being completely supportive of yourself. Give yourself a compliment, notice something nice about yourself and give yourself a kind word. Try doing this for two hours, then one whole day, and then keep extending the time. When you see how much better you feel being self-supportive rather than self-destructive, you will never want to go back. But it takes practice. You have to overcome all those beliefs about yourself that say "You have to change," "You are not good enough like you are," and so on. How silly such thoughts seem in an environment where self-support is the dominant feeling.

UNDERSTANDING OUR EMOTIONS

It is impossible to have two dominant thoughts at the same time. Therefore, as long as your thoughts are dominated by worry or fear, you can't feel happy. You can be *generally* happy and still experience negative emotions, too. But whenever negative emotions are allowed to dominate, the feeling of happiness is lost.

Notice how often we allow ourselves to become angry and how this cuts into our happiness. Imagine this: I am driving home on a snowy day. I am being very careful and am happy because the snow is beautiful and I am looking forward to sledding with my son. Suddenly a car loses control at an intersection and slides into the side of my car. My reaction is likely to be anger at the other driver, frustration at the delay, and nervousness because of the threat of serious injury. I may pause a moment to realize that I am OK and then charge out of the car to vent my emotions on the other driver. I may begin yelling and pointing at the damage to my car. I have lost all feeling of happiness, and I will only regain that feeling when I regain control over my emotions.

Some people would stay angry until the police came and even then would continue to yell and carry on. They might even complain to the truck driver on the way to the garage and to all their friends when they get home. Their anger can last for days or weeks, depending on the time it takes to fix the car and settle insurance claims. In short, one minor accident can destroy a person's happiness for a long period of time. *But only if the person allows it to happen.*

It is important to understand that negative emotions are not totally controllable. Anyone can get upset by things like car accidents. The problem arises when you *dwell* on these negative feelings, feel guilty for having them, and maintain them for more than a few minutes. The idea is to be aware of your negative feelings; note that the source of those feelings is your own mind, and then choose to move on to something else. The key is to recognize that there is a choice and that the battle is between you and your mind. At first, it is hard to regain your composure and choose to forgive, forget, and move on. But a few victories over minor irritations show that it can be done. Then the idea is to face sterner and sterner tests of your ability to forget and move on.

PRACTICING EMOTIONAL SELF-CONTROL

We have said that people lose their happiness for extended periods of time because *they* allow self-destructive emotions to dominate their thoughts. The reason such emotions are triggered so readily is that people have similar defense mechanisms as other animals. Notice how a deer can be running at full speed the very instant it detects danger.

That reaction is instinctive. Human nature causes people to flare up in anger or fear almost instantly when they feel challenged too. The difference between people and animals is that people can use their mind to control their reactions. Animals can't think — they can only react.

People will act just as animals if they do not practice control over their emotions. Without practice, people are quick to anger. Let's look at another example. I suffered for years from the tensions of driving in rush hour traffic. I would change from lane to lane, get impatient, and stay really tense — sometimes long after I reached my destination. I thought this behavior was "natural" because after all, almost everyone did it. One day I learned that such behavior was "natural," but not necessary. What a relief. All I had to do was practice self control. I had to train myself to remain calm. Sure enough, it worked. It worked when I *anticipated* being caught in traffic and told myself to remain calm.

If you *anticipate* traffic tie-ups, criticism, failures, and other potentially upsetting events, you can easily learn to handle them without getting upset. Try it. Say to yourself firmly that tomorrow when you get caught in traffic, you will remain calm and think pleasant thoughts. Plan to stay in one lane, take your time, and relax. Of course you will have to plan to leave a little earlier "just in case." If you do this diligently, you will immediately eliminate much of the tension of driving. You can sit back, play some music, and enjoy the drive. You can do the same with criticism and failures of all kind. Plan for them to happen and plan your reaction. You will find you will have much more control.

But watch out for this: You plan to leave early but something delays you. You may suddenly revert to your old tense behavior. This may happen when you receive *unexpected* criticism or fail *unexpectedly.* Instantly, instinctively, you may become upset. Can you ever stop such feelings? Probably not, but you can minimize the time that such feelings dominate.

It is important to recognize that *you* are the cause of your feelings. Practice playing the part of a person who is not upset. At first, it will take you a long time to get into the part. But do it again with the next problem and the next. Use your meditation technique to calm your mind. Soon you will lessen the time it takes to get into the part of the cool, collected observer. With *much* practice and many setbacks, you can get to the point where the calm reaction is almost instantaneous. You can shorten the learning time by imagining such situations and visualizing yourself being calm and controlled.

PRACTICING SELF SUPPORT

Turning to others is something many of us have been practicing all of our lives that we must unlearn. We love to have others give us praise, and hate to have them criticize us. We have all played the game of mutual support for years. We are very good at it. Sometimes it seems to work quite well.

But there are serious dangers in playing that game. We learn to rely on others to *make us feel* good. When we are young and strong and good looking, the support comes often. But by allowing others to bolster our feelings, we give them equal power to crush our feelings. And it happens sooner or later; our looks fade or our athletic ability falls off some. People notice, they comment, and we feel crushed. We then try to play the game better. We put on more makeup or lose weight or study books. But it is never enough, others just don't praise us often enough.

Giving others the power *to make us feel good or to make us feel bad* is a very destructive game. But because we feel so good when we get support from others it's often very difficult to give up. With practice, it's possible to replace that need for support with *self-*support.

Notice the times when others *make you* feel bad. Really

experience the agony it causes. Then tell yourself you hate that feeling. Do it again, and again, and again. Soon you will have a string of put downs and criticisms that will make you furious. So, get furious! Really experience how resentful you feel. Then vow with all your emotions never to let that happen again. Free yourself from the *reliance* on others. Say things like "I don't need praise to know I'm good," or "I will never again let others dictate my happiness." Practice over and over in your mind. Program it into your mind.

If you find yourself slipping and desiring support from others, repeat the process above. Review the lesson on stroking yourself until you have mastered it. And vow never again to get caught up in the "mutual support" game.

I imagine your mind is going crazy over this concept. Mine did. Most of us feel that mutual support is what makes life worth living, and there is a bit of truth in that. Everyone wants to love and be loved. But we should never let ourselves be put in the position of being addicted to mutual support. Only from a base of self-reliance can we give and receive support without fear of losing it. The support of others then *adds to,* but is not the *cause of* our happiness.

After you have learned this lesson well, notice how it works with children. Children grow fastest when we give them minimum support and allow them to develop *self reliance.* But isn't it "right" to want to help your own child? It may *seem* right, but you know that it is really destructive of their ability to manage their own life, their own happiness, and their own sadness.

Oh, how I wrestle with these thoughts. I want so much to protect and help my son. He is so young, so vulnerable. But if I am not there to protect him, he will be on his own. So I must let him grow to be strong on his own. I am practicing letting him be. I need more practice. I am practicing stroking others and my *Self.* I need more practice. I will need to practice the rest of my life, or until I master my *Self.*

THE HAPPINESS GAME

EXERCISES FOR DEVELOPING SELF-RELIANCE AND SELF SUPPORT

Only through practice can we learn self control. Here are some exercises that will help you gain that skill.

1. Make a 100% commitment to practicing.
2. Create a clear image in your mind of *who* you are growing to be and *how* you will behave when you get there.
3. Write down your behaviors that need developing.
4. Practice acting like the person you are growing to be for 10 minutes a day. Practice being outgoing, assertive, loving, and kind. Practice "stroking" others during those 10 minutes. After a few days, increase the time to 20 minutes. Working at your own pace, step up the time until you *become* that person you've been playing.
5. Practice stroking your Self. Do it for a few minutes each morning before the mirror. Give yourself love and approval. When you feel comfortable doing that, increase the time until you feel self-supportive all day long.
6. Practice self-control using the following steps:
   a. Notice the situations when you feel angry and upset.
   b. Practice being calm during those situations in your mind. Think through them as if you were there, but imagine acting calm, and collected. *Anticipate* the next frustrating incident and notice how you can control your reactions.
   c. Notice when anger occurs sometimes when you least expect it. Notice that it is not the *event* that caused the upset, but *your reaction to it.*

Developing Happiness Skills through Practice

d. Focus on playing the role of a calm person. Work on this until you can cut the time you remain upset to a few minutes at most.

PLAYING TODAY'S GAME TODAY

Imagine trying to play a game with someone who is not concentrating. You might notice that the person seems to make a lot of mistakes. When you ask what is happening, the person replies, "I'm sorry, I was just thinking how badly I played yesterday. I could have played so much better. I can't believe I screwed up so badly." Naturally, you'd want that person to forget about yesterday's game. As long as he's reliving that game in his mind, he can't be totally here with you and the game you're playing now won't be any fun.

Imagine further that because of his lack of attention your opponent is losing. You know he still has the potential for winning and you are eager to continue. But, he wants to give up. If he goes on, he might lose and he doesn't want to lose. Of course, in that case you can't win either. And winning is fun, as long as the game is played fairly and there is no *need* to win.

But your opponent begins worrying about tomorrow's game. He talks about how he will overcome the obstacles tomorrow and how tomorrow he is sure he'll win. How frustrating! Wouldn't you love to scream, "Look, the only game that counts is the one you're playing *now!* Yesterday's game is over; there is nothing you can do about it now. Tomorrow's game is tomorrow. You can't play it now. The only game that is real is this one."

Getting in the game now is a basic skill in the happiness game. And it takes practice.

DON'T MAKE COMPARISONS

Have you ever analyzed how much of your time you spend reliving exciting times in the past or anticipating exciting times in the future? Occasional daydreaming is fine; it can help generate nice thoughts on an otherwise dull day. But some people spend most of their time reliving the past or planning the future and, therefore, lose the *now*.

Today can be just as fun, just as interesting, and just as rewarding as yesterday or tomorrow. But today tends to lose its own special joys when it is compared to something else. For example, some time in our lives we may experience a perfect day at the beach. The sun is just right, the water is clean and cool and we feel great! It's a tremendous high to be alive on such a day and to experience all the bodily sensations that go with it. But analyzing, or comparing, or worrying about what we *should be* doing can spoil the nice day.

As soon as we try to intellectualize an event, the event loses its special meaning and becomes a thought rather than an experience. It's not that we should not think while having pleasant experiences; rather, we shouldn't allow thoughts to *overcome* our feelings. For example, many married couples can remember the time when being together, sharing sex, and just talking were joyous occasions. Every moment crackled with pleasure. To capture such feelings, people get married and prepare for a life full of pleasure. But soon they find that communication loses some of its special qualities and sex becomes routine. One major cause of such a letdown is that couples compare experiences rather than live them for what they are *now*. They ask themselves, almost subconsciously: Is this sexual experience what it once was? Is it what I expected? Are we as happy as others? Do we have as much fun, have sex as often, have as many friends, do as many things, read as many books, make as much money?

By comparing and analyzing, we ruin our enjoyment of now. We can never live up to the standards of the world. Someone else can always make more money and have more fun. So to really enjoy the present, we must stop comparing and analyzing. Sex is great now, period! We're having fun now, period! What makes one experience great and another boring is your attitude. And since you control your attitude, you can control your experiences. You can make today a highlight of your life. After all, you're alive, you're reading this book, and you can see. That alone make today great!

Comparing your experiences with other people's also ruins your enjoyment of now. Was my party as fun as Helen's? Am I as good in bed as your first husband? If comparisons can ruin a great day at the beach and sex, think how it can ruin your feelings toward a new job or a quiet day when life is what it is and not a spectacular event.

The last thing that can destroy today, no matter how good today is, is thinking about what you *should* be doing. Even a beautiful day at the beach can be ruined by constantly thinking about the things left undone at home. You have one main responsibility in life — *to live it*. And to play the happiness game, there is only one dominant obligation in life: you should live every day fully and enjoy it. A life full of joy will give you the energy to do what you want to do, including what you should do, if you so choose.

With that perspective, we can help others and assume responsibilities. Not because we *should,* but because a natural outgrowth of enjoying ourselves is to share with others and to be responsible. But our first responsibility is to ourselves. We cannot be loving to others without first being loving to ourselves. The most important obligation then, is allowing ourselves to be happy and to spread that happiness to others.

KEEPING IN THE NOW

One rather fun exercise for staying in the now is playing the role of uninvolved observer. Watch yourself acting out the day. Notice how your mind wanders to past events and future hopes. Watch what you do and how you do it. And notice what causes you anger, fear, love and jealousy. Don't evaluate, just observe. This exercise allows your mind to do its thing while you stay in the now. Soon your mind will notice the game you are playing and will want to play too. What you should strive for is meditation all day long, not just 20 minutes in the morning and afternoon.

During any given day, you have multiple occasions to practice being in the now: dressing, eating breakfast, driving to work, working, eating lunch, driving home, eating dinner, watching television, reading. Did you ever analyze why we get so upset when our shoelace breaks, when traffic is slow, or when service is slow at a restaurant? We are in a hurry! We almost always want to *be* somewhere else. But we can never *be* anywhere but here, now. Silly, isn't it? You can meditate all day long by focusing on your own rushing. Notice it, laugh at it, get into it deeply, and return to the now fun of being aware again.

HAPPINESS VERSUS THRILLS

One reason so few people find lifelong happiness is because they confuse happiness with excitement, thrills, or bliss. Happiness is not usually as intense as all that. Happiness can include such intense feelings but is not dependent upon them. Happiness is acceptance of *what is* (choosing what you have) and *what is* may be simply all right. But we cannot run away from what is, because running away prevents awareness of the now. Running away is not moving up, it is moving sideways. To move up, we must stop running, notice where we are, accept where we are as the Truth, and then begin the climb. There is no other way to go up than to begin with *now*. Basing growth on fantasies and hopes is an exercise in futility. Find happiness in the now; then you can move up. To hold on to it, simply live moment to moment and make the most of what is.

PROBLEMS WITH LIVING FROM HIGH TO HIGH

Often people get off the road to happiness by taking side trips that lead to temporary "highs." It certainly adds to the enjoyment of life experiencing the excitement of downhill ski racing; canoeing down the rapids; or making love with an exciting new lover. But the diversions too often become goals and people become addicted to excitement. They feel "low" unless they are "high." Sometimes the quickest high comes from drugs. Drugs have caused the ruin of many people.

The problem with living from high to high is that the middle is often very depressing. Furthermore, people become so used to highs that the highs begin to lose the punch they had at first. Consequently, they have to find even greater thrills in order to be happy. No matter how carefully they plan though, the end will always be the same — the high goes away. How pathetic are those who become addicted to such thrills.

Thrills are not anything like happiness! Happiness is steady, while thrills are up and down. Happiness is quiet and pleasureful, while thrills are loud and heart pounding. Certainly a happy person can experience periodic thrills, but that is not the goal. Thrills are strictly sidelights to a more assured happiness.

HAPPINESS IN MANY SMALL PLEASURES

Rather than seeking happiness in the temporary thrills of life, you should look for ways to make the here and now more enjoyable. Rather than seeking lots of excitement, seek a relaxed satisfaction with life.

Your goal is to develop a base of happiness from which you can proceed through life. That base of happiness is built upon the small pleasures of everyday living — a smile from a friend, a pleasant song, a gentle breeze, or a bird singing. Sometimes people miss these small pleasures on the way to finding thrills. Meditation enables you to stop during the day and let your mind relax so that it can recapture the joys of small pleasures. If you feel that life today is a drag, you are probably missing the fun of being in touch with yourself and your environment.

To get the most out of the daily game of life, we must practice making optimum use of all our senses. The world is full of wonderful sounds, smells, sights, tastes, and textures. But our senses become dulled over time and only through conscious effort can we regain our childlike sense of wonder about the things around.

THE PLEASURES OF TASTE

In the hustle and bustle of 20th century living, many of us view meals as a necessary evil to be disposed of as quickly as possible. Our breakfast may be toast and coffee, lunch a sandwich and soft drink, and dinner the only meal where we relax and enjoy it. But such a casual attitude toward food has a tendency to dull our sense of taste until many of us actually prefer hamburgers and french fries to more exotic meats, wines and delicate sauces.

An important skill in the happiness game, therefore, is to rediscover the variety of taste sensations that many of us have lost. What we eat is mostly a matter of habit, so we can begin to appreciate food more by consciously planning our meals to give ourselves variety. We all have certain meals that we consider special taste treats. For example, I really look forward to Thanksgiving when the family gets together for turkey, dressing, whipped potatoes, special salads and desserts. But why should Thanksgiving be the only day for such a delicious meal? After all, turkey is relatively inexpensive, and the rest of the meal not too difficult to prepare. Why not plan Thanksgiving-type meals several times a year? My family does this, and I really enjoy it.

Developing Happiness Skills through Practice

96

What other foods do you enjoy? Roasts, ham, fish, or what? Rather than waiting until the last minute to plan meals, why not plan menus for an entire week? Any why not have at least one special meal each day? If you plan for it ahead of time, preparation of a special meal takes little more time than routine meals. But remember, you must take time to enjoy these meals after you prepare them!

One way to broaden your taste sense is to eat in different restaurants. Each person can share a portion of his meal with everyone else. This way you can try a wide variety of foods at a very low cost and learn what you like and do not like. Try to be open minded about this at first because if you think you won't like something, you probably won't. That is your beliefs playing games with you again.

Why not take a few minutes now to list the foods you enjoy? Go ahead, write them down. Notice any taste treats you have been missing lately? Plan now to buy the ingredients and enjoy that meal. And don't forget to eat those meals more slowly! Meals are a great time to practice enjoying the now.

MY FAVORITE FOODS:

_____

_____

_____

_____

_____

_____

_____

_____

_____

_____

THE HAPPINESS GAME

FAVORITE FOODS OF OTHERS
I REGULARLY EAT WITH:

_____

_____

_____

_____

_____

_____

_____

_____

_____

_____

_____

THE PLEASURES OF AROMAS AND SCENTS

A large part of taste is actually smell. For example, an onion gets its flavor from its scent rather than its taste. Try tasting an onion while holding your nose. Try the same experiment with coffee and other foods and you will learn the relationship between tastes and smells.

Concern about body odors has caused most Americans to try to eliminate rather than accent their sense of smell. But with just a little effort you will find whole new experiences in basic scents. You can begin by smelling, not tasting, different wines.

All of us have experienced the pleasant fragrance of a rose. But, did you know different roses have different fragrances? Go into a rose garden and explore the variety of aromas. Or while riding on a bicycle, notice the many smells you miss while riding in an enclosed car: the smell of new-mown grass, the pungent smell of wild onions, the pleasant scent of pine trees and honeysuckle vines, and the offensive odors of dead skunks. On rainy days, explore the scents of your home by smelling the pleasant aroma of coffee, spices, and perfumes. These experiences are just an introduction to a whole new world of scents.

By consciously exploring the wide world of smells, you will take new delight when passing a bakery, a tobacco shop, or an old barn. The scents of every meal and every long walk will add to your happiness. Remember your goal is to practice keeping your mind focused on the now so that you get optimum pleasure out of each moment.

THE PLEASURES OF SIGHT

One of my favorite occupations is to sit at an intersection and watch the people go by. I can spend hours concentrating on different things about people: how they walk, what they wear, how they wear their hair.

Learning to see all the beauty of the world takes practice too. We all have a tendency to look and not see, see and not understand, or understand and not assimilate. To really appreciate a fine painting or a mountain view, we must learn to concentrate on the particular as well as the whole. Separate colors, images, and parts can be appreciated as much or more than the whole. One bird in flight can raise our spirits as much as a whole flock. But we must learn to look for beauty and to *see* for the first time many of the things that before had seemed ordinary.

Many of us have a tendency to look only for the unusual, and therefore miss the ordinary. But in the ordinary, there is much that is unusual and different if we would only look. People from all over the country flocked to see the new Mormon Temple when it was built in

Maryland. Yet there are beautiful churches all over the country that the local people have never seen. We will often travel thousands of miles to see something that is available in our own back yard. In our search for the forest, we fall over the trees. In our search for the most beautiful, we pass up the beautiful.

Try to see more of the great and the beautiful in everything you see. Try it for a few minutes each day and eventually it will become a habit and the world will look better to you because *you* changed. Where there is *real* ugliness and filth around you, do something about it! Pick up the litter, plant some flowers, and next time you go that way things will be that much better.

THE GLORY OF SOUNDS

Have you opened yourself to all the different sounds of the world? Have you listened to the music of the Orient, the symphonies of the Europeans, the jazz of the American South? As with all our senses, we have a tendency to listen to the same kind of music all of the time and ignore the other forms. But we then cut ourselves off from new sounds, new experiences, and the potential for raising our levels of enjoyment far beyond our present limits.

There is music in everything we do if we would only stop and listen. There is even joy in listening to the sounds of silence. It gives us a sense of peacefulness.

The sound of birds singing may arouse the same passions as a symphony orchestra if we listen with the same intensity. Combine the sounds of birds with the whistling of the wind, the rustling of leaves, and the babbling of a brook and you have nature's symphony being played at its finest. And the cost is right!

I find great happiness in singing. I wish two things for my son, two things that have brought me great happiness — a love for music and a sense of humor. I get great inspiration from these words of Santayana: "To be happy was to sing; not to be made to sing; not to sing by rote, or as an art for a purpose, but spontaneously, religiously, because something sang within you and all else for the moment was remote and still."

THE PLEASURES OF TOUCH

Many of us touch things throughout the day, but rarely do we really feel them. The cold, hard feel of steel contrasts with the warm, soft surface of a textured sofa. The feel of highly polished wood contrasts with the feel of a wool shirt.

But even when we do touch items around us, we tend to use fingers calloused by constant abuse. Try placing a piece of steel on your forehead. Notice how cold it seems; how hard. Now place a piece of wood against your forehead. Notice how much warmer and softer it feels compared to the steel.

Close your eyes and become aware of the sensations on the surface of your body. Notice how your shoes feel. Feel how your clothing brushes against your legs. Feel the tightness around your waist. Notice how your jewelry feels against your skin. Feel the temperature of the room.

Learn to use your sense of touch in combination with the other senses. Pick up a lemon and feel the outer surface. Then taste the peel, the seeds, the juice, and the pulp. Smell the difference between the peel and the pulp. Begin to experience all foods this completely.

Taking time to discover such small pleasures makes you more full of curiosity and excitement. The everyday becomes unusual. Your meals become a total body sensation rather than a mere feeding of the machine.

EXERCISES FOR
INCREASING SENSUAL AWARENESS

To gain more appreciation for the gift of our senses, try doing this. Imagine for a moment that you are going blind and have only one week left to see. Spend an entire day looking at things as if you might never see them again. Study the faces of your family and friends and remember the color of their eyes, the shape of their nose, and the flow of their hair. Take a walk through the woods with the thought that *this is the last time* I will ever see these things. Get up early and watch the sunrise. Watch the sunset. Walk through your neighborhood and look at things so that you will never forget them. Notice during these exercises how much more beauty and interest you can find when you really look.

The next day spend your time listening to the sounds of life. Again, walk through the woods and your neighborhood. Notice all the sounds you missed the day before when you were concentrating on seeing. Listen to the sound of your friends' voices. Listen to a recording of a symphony orchestra. Listen for the individual instruments and how they blend with others. Do the same with a bluegrass record and a jazz record. Then notice the sound of silence. Listen carefully to silence and imagine that being all you will ever hear again.

Spend the next day using your sense of smell to its fullest. Smell your food, your neighborhood and take a third walk through the woods. Notice how many odors you missed during the first two walks.

Once you have practiced opening your senses, you can experiment with your feelings. Notice what sensations come up when you dwell on the following:

> your spouse (or closest friend)
> your mother and father
> your job
> vacations

Developing Happiness Skills through Practice

your friends
TV
sports
sex
food
dogs
violence
your enemies

Devote a few minutes to each subject. Just close your eyes and let your thoughts come. Experience all the emotions that come up — anger, love, disappointment, passion, and jealousy. Note that each emotion is different and *adds* to your experience. No emotion is good or bad, it is just part of living.

Notice, too, that you can emote various feelings at will. Go through the list again and notice how each word allows you to generate a new feeling. If you want to generate a different feeling, *think about something else*. It is just as simple or just as hard as *you* make it. Take time to make maximum use of your feelings as you do with each of your senses: sight, smell, and so forth.

After you have practiced the above exercises, life need never be dull for you. Whenever you become bored, you can concentrate on using your senses more fully to get more out of what you are doing. If that does not work, close your eyes and mentally reconstruct the list of things to think about. Leave out the things that trigger unpleasant feelings and dwell on those that trigger pleasant sensations. Time spent waiting for doctors or buses can become opportunities to get in touch with life again through tuning up your senses.

THE HAPPINESS GAME

103

AN EXERCISE TO DEVELOP LIVING IN THE NOW

Here are the ways to develop the skill of living in the now.

1. Look at each event in your life as a new game (an event is a trip to the beach, a visit from a friend, or a day at work).

2. Live that event moment by moment and don't compare it with any other event. Experience all the emotions that arise: boredom, excitement, anger, fear, etc. Notice that the event just is and you create your own reactions.

3. Within the event, try to create a new emotion. For example, concentrate more on what is happening and try to change your boredom to interest and then to excitement.

4. Note your ability to create a different feeling at will. Then write down on a piece of paper: Events just are; it is my attitude that makes them fun or not. Choose to make events fun and they will be.

5. Continue practicing the sensual awareness exercises in this chapter.

6. Notice that excitement and thrills are not the same as happiness. Enjoy them when they come, but don't seek them as substitutes for happiness. Rather, build a base of happiness and then let the excitement of special events add to it.

SCORING THE GAME

Let's pause now to see how well developed your happiness skills are. Do you need more practice? Score yourself from 1 to 10 depending on how accurately the following statements describe you — 1 means "not at all" and 10 means "perfectly."

LIVING IN THE NOW!

Statements	Now	After 6 Months	After 1 Year
1. I am open to new experiences.	5		
2. I practice stroking myself and others every day.	5		
3. I am willing to play the part of a person even more joyful and happy than I am now.	9		
4. I notice that the *cause* of my anger is my mind.	9		
5. I do not judge myself by the opinions of others.	2		
6. I am enjoying what I am doing now — reading this book and writing down my scores.	8		
7. I am not comparing this experience with any other experience in my life.	–		
8. My choices in life are not dominated by what I should or should not do.			
9. I make optimum use of my senses.			
10. I do not long for more thrills in life, but I enjoy them when they come.	1		
Total Score			

Starting Date _____

THE HAPPINESS GAME

105

Chapter 6

Playing with Enthusiasm

A child usually reacts to the announcement that the family is off to the circus with excitement and enthusiasm. Children feel enthusiastic often; adults less often. Therefore, to increase our joy, we need to recapture the childlike enthusiasm that many of us have lost.

What is it that makes children enthusiastic? It's doing what we like. (You should refer to your list in Chapter Two).

THE POWER OF ENTHUSIASM

Enthusiasm is contagious. It comes from Greek words that mean "full of God." Enthusiastic people have the power to fill others with the same spirit they have. The spirit comes from a child-like surrender to the wonder and magic of life. That same spirit pervades the individual so that he or she gets full measure out of every experience. If you want to be enthusiastic, you can start by associating with enthusiastic people.

Note how much enjoyment certain announcers add to a sports event. Every play is presented as an exciting element in an even more exciting game. If you are away from the TV set, an announcer can make you race back into the TV room to watch the replay of a minor event during the game. What causes that excitement? Enthusiasm! It's contagious. Think of how dull a game becomes when the sound goes off. You are left with your own reactions and some of the excitement is lost. That is why attending a game in person is so much more exciting than watching it on TV.

When I was a bachelor, I dated many different young women. Some were athletic, some were pretty and still others were sexy. But one young woman had something that surpasses beauty and all other traits. That something is enthusiasm. At the time I had a motorcycle, and this person would ride on the back and be thrilled by a ride in the country. When we would go to a movie or restaurant or anything else, this young woman approached the event enthusiastically. Her enthusiasm was so contagious that I enjoyed everything I did with her. My life was better with her than without her. Fortunately, I was able to marry her, and my life has been much fuller ever since. Now we have a young son, and my wife's enthusiasm has worn off on him. What a joy it is to be with him. His spirit pervades the whole house and fills us all with joy.

It is not easy being enthusiastic. But like everything else in life,

Playing with Enthusiasm

enthusiasm can be learned. You must act *as if* you are enthusiastic. Make it a game. Soon that part will become natural to you. To support that feeling, surround yourself with other enthusiastic people and you will feed on each other. Soon you will wonder what happened to that complacent person you once were.

My neighbor, Hillary, is someone who used sleep as an escape mechanism. She found it very difficult to get out of bed some mornings, and, like me, she periodically got sleepy during the day. Some days there just wasn't anything to get enthusiastic about. Here are a few things she did to invigorate herself:

1. When you wake up in the morning, ignore how your body feels and get mentally involved in something fun. Get out of bed, take a shower, and immerse yourself in a project that you enjoy doing. You will find that once your mind is ready to go your body will follow. Hillary puts it this way, "Don't wait until you feel like doing something, *just do it* and you will feel 100% better and wide awake."
2. Take out that list of things you enjoy doing. Get involved in one of those things whenever you feel sleepy or get involved in *planning* something fun. *Having energy is a choice; it comes when we choose to get involved.*
3. Call up an enthusiastic person and talk about their latest fun project. Let their enthusiasm wear off on you.

GLOOM IS CONTAGIOUS TOO

Just as an enthusiastic person can affect other people, so too can a gloomy person. "You become whom you associate with" is the rule. If you run around with losers, you are likely to become a loser too.

My friend, Steve, had a thirteen year old son. The son was intelligent, but he was not doing well in school. Steve felt his son had tremendous potential, but was not living up to it. Steve told his friend Jeff about his problem. Jeff's son was the same age as Steve's and was very successful in both school and athletics. Steve decided to visit his friend Jeff more often and bring his son with him. The boys could play while their dads talked. Soon the boys became friends and spent more time together. In one year, Steve's son changed into a successful student and athlete. He gave up his old neighborhood gang.

Steve still marvels over the power of a boy's peers to influence his life. His son had let his friends lead him to become indifferent about school and athletics. He had followed the group's norms in dress, behavior, and attitudes, but when Chris was introduced to a new, more positive lifestyle, he took to it immediately. He rejected his old friends and took on the values and attitudes of his new friend.

Many parents have learned that friends influence children's lives more completely than parents do. This influence is great if the peer group is motivated. But if the peer group is hostile and unmotivated, these behaviors are passed along. Gloom breeds gloom, hatred breeds hatred, and indifference breeds indifference. A whole group can be affected by one dominant anti-social person.

Young people aren't the only ones influenced by their peers. Adults also learn to love or hate what their peers love and hate. Whole blocks can become bigoted and whole neighborhoods can become centers of distrust and crime. The feeling can spread throughout an entire city until it begins to affect the mood of the nation.

Notice how pessimistic the people in the U.S. are today. They are disillusioned with education, government, business, medicine, and all other establishment organizations. This is true in spite of the fact that we are experiencing freedom from war, improving health, and the highest education level ever. Gloom breeds gloom and the newspapers, magazines, and TV pick up the theme and spread it like the plague.

Playing with Enthusiasm

Soon we all become infected and join others in attacking authority. Listen to the conversations at a party and note how often the subject being discussed is corrupt politicians, uncaring landlords, or overpaid actors or athletes. Before you know it, you too are joining the "nay sayers" and attacking the world and everyone in it.

If you want to feel happy and optimistic, you must avoid "nay sayers" as much as possible. Seek the company of the truly gifted people; those the nay sayers are usually against. Become involved with concerned citizens who are doing positive things to improve situations. Attend a church or synagogue where the spiritual leaders are truly inspirational people. Life will seem much more positive when you associate with positive people. The nation will still have its ups and downs, but you will rise above the national miasma to become your own optimistic and self-assured person.

OVERCOMING BOREDOM

To get the most out of the happiness game, we must also learn to overcome bordom. Some people are bored all the time — with their spouse, their job, and their friends. But like most of our problems in life, boredom is an *attitude*, not a fact of life.

When we first moved to Maryland, we met a couple from Colorado. They were very interested in nature and loved hiking and camping. My wife and I were city folk and not interested in "roughing it." When this couple invited us to go bird watching with them, our first reactions were, "How boring." But we were even more bored doing what we had been doing and decided to give bird watching a chance. Well, that was the first of many bird watching trips! Now these trips are some of our favorite activities.

This couple also introduced us to white water rafting. We hesitated at first because it meant getting wet, paddling for hours, living in a tent and cooking out. But we went anyhow and absolutely loved it.

Before we got involved with bird watching and other outdoor activities, we thought of outdoors people as "boring" because they never talked about anything except their adventures. We were more interested in talking about good restaurants, plays and travel. Now we share their enthusiasm and really enjoy talking about it!

My wife and I learned a lot from our Colorado friends. We learned that no person or activity is boring unless we make it so. But often in the past we had shut out people because their interests were different. We tended to associate with people with the same interests and backgrounds as ourselves. Now we see that everybody is interesting if you give them a chance to share *their* interests in *their own way*.

Think of the millions of people in the United States who find ballet, fishing and classical music boring. Rather than open themselves to new experiences, they stick with the same interests they have followed all their lives. And they find ballet enthusiasts and fishermen boring when they talk so lovingly about their interests. Life is truly boring when people shut themselves off from new experiences and friends because they are not interested in *new* things.

Therefore the first step toward making life more interesting is to develop a new attitude toward others. That attitude is: *No one is boring*. Everyone has an interest in something we know little about and by probing deeply we can find new interests. Even people who seem to do nothing all day can be interesting, no doubt they have interesting attitudes toward life and work.

If you find yourself bored at parties, ask yourself why you are allowing yourself to become bored. Then approach the next person or event completely open. Don't make any pre-judgments, listen, probe, and get as deeply involved as possible. You will find excitement in every person, if you allow it to happen.

Playing with Enthusiasm

FAITH IN GOD

There are times when some people feel so low that life does not seem worth living. These people are so despondent that relief comes only from alcohol or drugs. Often they turn away from almost everyone and everything and turn inward to find some trace of meaning. When a person relies totally on himself or herself for all that is good and desirable in life, there is no place to go when everything falls to pieces. When that happens, the individual at times begins to consider suicide or his or her mind might give relief through a breakdown.

Who can these people turn to for help and inspiration? Usually they are so estranged from their families that communication is impossible. Their friends have often tried their best, but have given up in their struggle to help. Professional therapists are often too expensive or too impersonal to trust. But there is someone who respects everyone's feelings even when things seem too awful to share. God is the counselor of last resort. God is willing to listen, understand, and offer the kind of guidance that people who have hit bottom need.

One of the better stories I have read on the theme, "I'm a success, why aren't I happy?" was written by Charles Colson, one of President Nixon's closest aides. He describes his climb up the career ladder from being valedictory of his class in school, to turning down Harvard for Brown University, to joining the Marines, to law school at George Washington University, to joining the staff of the President. Colson's book, *Born Again,* describes the deadness of spirit he felt at the moment when he should have been experiencing his greatest victory. Colson had been addicted to pride, and pride had led him to do all kinds of unethical things which eventually led to a prison term. But long before his fall, Colson felt an uneasy feeling of the "I'm a success, why aren't I happy?" variety.

During his period of self-analysis, Colson met Tom Phillips who was then the President of the Raytheon Company. Tom Phillips changed Colson's life. Phillips shared with Colson his feelings that his life "wasn't worth anything" even though he was president of a huge industrial firm, had a beautiful home, a Mercedes, a great family, and everything a person could want, *except happiness.* Tom Phillips found happiness by commiting his life to God. It was spirituality that was missing from his life. Once he found his spiritual life, he was both successful and happy. Colson was haunted by the conversation with Tom Phillips about how his commitment to God changed his life. Eventually, Colson made a similar commitment.

If you are saying, "I'm a success, why aren't I happy?", perhaps what is missing in your life is a commitment to God. That means letting God into your life as counselor and friend. It means serving God and others. You'll never know how happy God can make you unless you give your spiritual life a chance.

PRAYER WORKS

Whenever you have problems or questions you want help with, always begin with prayer. The act of praying itself does much to solve your problems. First, prayer gets you to analyze the problem so that you know better what it is you want. Second, prayer makes you forget about yourself for a minute and allows you to see the problem from the perspective of an outsider — God. Third, prayer is the first step toward doing something about the problem. It makes you verbalize the problem, think of solutions, and overcome the inertia of not doing anything. Prayer works. Prayer will lead you back to the now. It will give you new confidence in yourself.

LIFE IS RENEWED AT FORTY

The age of forty seems to be a milestone in many people's lives. As we approach forty, we start to realize that we are getting older and that middle age has arrived. For many of us, this realization is traumatic, and it triggers feelings of doubt and despair (the mid-life crisis). Rather than being enthusiastic about the wonderful years ahead, we tend to look back at unaccomplished goals in the past.

At forty, life is ready to be renewed. It is a time when knowledge, ability and experience, are ready to be channelled into new projects. Charles Colson, Tom Phillips, Fred, and myself were about 40 when we found our new outlook on life.

Many people do not realize their full potential until even older than forty. Golda Meir was voted "the most admired woman" at the age of 71. People of all ages enjoy Kentucky Fried Chicken thanks to Colonel Sanders who was 65 when he took his delicious chicken to the world. Laura Ingalls Wilder, famous writer of children's books, began writing in her 60s. Sophocles wrote Oedipus Rex when he was 75, and Agatha Christie was in her mid 80s when she was turning out popular crime stories. Benjamin Franklin was 69 when he participated in the drafting of the Declaration of Independence, in his 70s when he was Ambassador to France, and a member of the Constitutional Convention at 81.

I could go on and on listing others who did not make a major contribution until late in life. Life may not begin at forty, but it sure takes on new and exciting dimensions. Fifty is a great time to finally "put it all together" and make some serious contributions to mankind. The same is true for people in their 60s, 70s, 80s, and 90s. The secret to a rewarding life at all ages is maintaining enthusiasm.

SCORING THE GAME

I'm enthusiastic about playing the happiness game and I hope my enthusiasm rubs off on you. Just how enthusiastic are you about life? Score yourself from 1 to 10 depending on how accurately you feel the following statements describe you: 1 means the statement does not describe you at all, 10 means it describes you perfectly.

HOW ENTHUSIASTIC ARE YOU ABOUT LIFE?

Statements	Your Score	Your Score After 6 Months	Your Score After 1 Year
1. I am enthusiastic about life.	_____	_____	_____
2. I feel everyone has something to say that is interesting.	_____	_____	_____
3. I know that happiness is possible at any age.	_____	_____	_____
4. My friends are full of joy and enthusiasm.	_____	_____	_____
5. I rarely discuss gloomy subjects with others.	_____	_____	_____
6. I do not make myself bored.	_____	_____	_____
7. I am happy with my spiritual beliefs.	_____	_____	_____
8. I have experienced the power of prayer.	_____	_____	_____
9. I do not mind talking or thinking about God and spiritual matters.	_____	_____	_____
10. I share my enthusiasm with others.	_____	_____	_____
Total Scores	_____	_____	_____

Starting Date _____

Playing with Enthusiasm

Chapter 7

Playing the Game with Love

*T*he importance of love in the happiness game cannot be overestimated. Yet there is probably no emotion less understood than love. First of all, there are so many different kinds of love: love of parent, love of spouse, love of pet, love of child, and love of mankind.

But what is love? Is love the same as passion and desire? Often people think it is, but we know that emotions come and go. Therefore, we could never promise to love forever if love were the same as passion. Passion comes and passion goes, but true love goes on steadily.

Is love a major *source* of happiness? No, love is a major

product of happiness. We should not seek happiness by developing loving relationships, rather, we should develop happiness and sharing that happiness will lead to loving relationships.

LOVE IS LETTING OTHERS BE

In the happiness game the definition of love is letting others be exactly what they are and what they are not. To show love, then, is to give others the freedom to be what they are.

Think of all the tension that would go out of family situations if people in the family would love each other as they are. From that base, all kinds of change is possible. But from a base of non-acceptance, little change can occur. Don't be stingy with your love and insist that others change to win it. If you're open, they will be too. In such an accepting atmosphere, people will naturally adapt to the wishes and feelings of others.

Children respond to love openly and quickly, so disciplining a child is easy when the base is love. But discipline is ineffective when the base is unacceptance. Accept your child's hair style, dress, and behavior in a loving manner. Don't expect your child to conform with what you want him to be. Rather, give children the freedom to be what they are and what they are not. In the end, you will find that all of you are better off.

A HAPPINESS TACTIC

One tactic to use in loving relationships is to notice all the things that irritate you about one particular person. Make a list of all their habits that irritate you. It could be that the person snores or squeezes the toothpaste incorrectly or throws dirty laundry on the floor. Then take the top 5 habits and forget them. That's right, *forget them*. Let them *be*. They can no longer be an irritant to you if you ignore them.

Then discuss this tactic with the other person. See if they will do the same for you. If annoying habits go away (and they will, if you let them be), then add others to your list to replace them. Try it; it works.

LOVE OF PARENT FOR A CHILD

The closest model to pure love in this world is the love of a parent toward his or her baby. A baby can do almost anything and still be loved. Love for a baby involves dirty diapers, sleepless nights, sickness, crying, and sacrifice of time and money. But all of that and more is part of parental love. Most parents allow their babies to be exactly as they are and are happy in that love.

This loving behavior of parents continues for several years. But around school age, some parents begin to change their attitudes. They want something in return for their love and attention; things like good grades, neatness and respect. Often they do not get what they want. This often results in less love of the child. Love for teenagers is often the ultimate test because teenagers actively seek freedom to be as they are. Parents often want their sons and daughters to meet their dream of what a teenager should be. Acceptance seems to fade, gulfs grow, pressures increase. What happened?

In short, the parents stopped fully loving them. Love is easier when it is an emotion. Parents can feel emotionally attached to children at all ages, but such attachment is not love; it is often the antithesis of love. Love is giving the child freedom; attachment is holding on. Love is letting them be; attachment is molding them to an image. Love is calm, cool, collected. Attachment is often frantic, passionate, and nerve wracking.

A parent who *loves* a child is quite willing to let that child go when the child is ready. Loving parents do not *need* their children around. Remember, love is allowing others freedom to fail, freedom to learn, and freedom from ties.

"Children came through you but not from you," writes Gibran, in *The Prophet,* "and though they are with you yet they belong not to you. You may strive to be like them, but seek not to make them like you."

LOVE IS GIVING

Love is a basic need for everyone. With love, people can learn to do without many niceties of life, but without love, life loses much meaning. But you may be wondering, "How can I find love when the world seems so full of indifference and nonacceptance?"

You cannot find love by seeking it for yourself. Love is the result of giving; you feel it when you offer it. Love reaches outward not inward, it happens when you stop concentrating on your own needs and desires and seek to fill the needs and desires of others, including their need to feel accepted as they are.

To find love, you should give something to every person you meet. "You give but little when you give your possessions," says Kahlil Gibran, in *The Prophet.* "It is when you give of yourself that you truly give." So when you give something to everyone you meet, you should give warmth, understanding, and time rather than material gifts. Those who give with love will get love in return. If the offer of Self is made with reserve or with a sense of loss, then the return will be small and the feeling of love lessened.

It is a risk to love because you open yourself to others and become vulnerable to their actions and attitudes. Therefore, love is an act of faith, and those who have little faith in others will have difficulty in experiencing it. Your life is fuller when you can love God, love your neighbor, and love yourself.

LOVE OF SELF COMES FIRST

"The affirmation of one's own life, happiness, growth, freedom," says Erich Fromm, in *The Art of Loving,* "is rooted in one's capacity to love." But Fromm also wrote that, "It is a widespread belief that, while it is virtuous to love others, it is sinful to love oneself." You must love yourself and be willing to give to yourself before you will have the capacity to give love to others.

Do you love yourself? Are you willing to give yourself the acceptance and understanding you are hoping to share with others? Often in our scramble to help others, we forget to look after ourselves. Out of a sense of duty, we will sacrifice our lives for another person only to find that the other person grows more demanding. That's because many people resent being given things when they cannot give in return. We can also feel it when others give out of a sense of duty rather than a sense of love. To correct this situation, we must first act for ourselves, and when our needs for self-fulfillment are satisfied, then and only then can we give more fully to others.

It is not being selfish to live and work for oneself. It is a necessary step toward giving to others. A person without food cannot nourish the hungry. A person without knowledge cannot give wisdom to others. And a person without love for Self cannot give love to others. Love, then, is really an expression of your self worth. The more you are able to give to others, the more you value yourself. To doubt yourself is to doubt others. To not trust yourself is to not trust others. But to be completely open with yourself is to be the same with others. And that comes from love.

THE HAPPINESS GAME

LOVING RELATIONSHIPS

I have learned that true love for another is at its fullest when both parties feel no need to change or manipulate the other. If one person in the relationship wants something from the other, that person should express that desire openly and clearly. But there should be total acceptance of the fact that the other *may* or *may not* respond to that request. Lovers *state* their needs; they do not demand that they be met. Lovers sometimes respond to the request of their partners and sometimes they do not. That is reality. To expect more is to expect love to do the impossible. *We do not always respond to our own needs; how can we expect others to be more responsive?*

Love assumes no obligations. The only obligation in a loving relationship is for both parties to be responsible for their *own* behavior and feelings. Loving support is *not* playing games or letting the other play games. Too often marriage partners play the dominant game, the submissive game or the irresponsible game. The only game that is mutually supportive is the happiness game — both partners seeking full expression of Self and assuming responsibility for Self.

What is your mind telling you about such a relationship? Does it seem strong? What holds it together? Where is the commitment? Where are the ties? This kind of relationship is unbelievably strong because mutual respect and acceptance hold it together.

There *is* much need for compromise in these relationships. Two people simply do not mesh perfectly in all things. But compromise cannot always be reached. How are such conflicts resolved? They are *not* resolved. A mature person must accept the fact that not all conflicts can be resolved. But doesn't that lead to frustration? Not unless the partners allow frustration to occur. Not always getting what we want is a fact of life, and if that is frustration, life is frustrating. But frustration is an opportunity to grow. Not getting one's way and taking responsibility for the feelings that come is a loving response. Resentment is not a loving response.

Love is an *ideal* — it is what we strive for. We may not embrace it completely, but we will come much closer if we understand it. We *can* learn to love our partners and our children and our government and even our enemies. Love is acceptance of what is.

LOVE BASED ON HAPPINESS

Love based on mutual self-satisfaction has great promise for deepening over time. Such love is based on two people who have a strong inner base of happiness. Because each partner is happy, the relationship is not *necessary* to them. Rather, the relationship is something extra; something beyond personal happiness. A loving relationship frees both partners from making demands. Furthermore, there is little anger or resentment generated if their desires occasionally go unfulfilled.

On the other hand, notice how much potential there is for getting what you want in such a relationship. Both partners need very little from each other, so both are free to be quite giving to one another. In this environment, love grows and grows. Since love is a basic need of everyone; this growth of love leads to even greater happiness, which promotes even more giving. A symbiotic relationship is formed that leads to further development for both parties. But notice the base: two people who are already happy and self-fulfilled.

LOVE THERAPY

Everyone needs love from the moment of birth. Children deprived of love are withdrawn and slow to develop. Love nurtures and heals. It is nature's finest medicine.

People are just now recognizing the restorative value of love. Children who have been deprived of love are given a cuddly dog to keep. The love shared by the child and dog brings out the best in both. Children become more verbal and aware. The more they can pour love out to their pet, the better they become.

Why is love so much easier between people and animals than between people? Because animals love their human companions with no reservations. They love them as they are. An animal's love is spontaneous and totally open. Love between people is more difficult. There is less spontaneity, less showing of true emotions, and less enthusiasm over time. A dog will jump for joy every day when its companion comes home. We should be so lucky to have the same response from our children, our spouse or our friends. To get that response, we have to be as accepting and as affectionate with them as we are with pets. The responsibility is ours!

SHOWING LOVE IS PART OF THE GAME

Love is more than passively letting others be, it must be expressed to be meaningful. Part of the happiness game is to express your love openly and spontaneously. Once you have clearly established a loving relationship with people, you must remain totally honest and open with them. That means telling them when they hurt you, telling them what you want, and listening to them when they express similar feelings. What takes the edge off of relationships is keeping feelings inside. That way, resentments build, and small irritants become magnified. When it does slip out, the truth comes out as an attack rather than a loving communication. To maintain a loving relationship, therefore, you should:

1. Be committed 100% to the relationship.
2. Keep all your agreements.
3. Express all your feelings openly and honestly *at the*

moment you feel them. (Don't try to hide negative thoughts or emotions; they will linger in your mind and are likely to come out later in a way that could damage the relationship).

4. Listen to others when they express their feelings and *thank* them for being open. Watch for body signals that indicate hidden feelings and encourage others to express what they feel.

5. Set aside a half hour each day for sharing, planning, and simply being with each other. That half hour should be completely yours, free from children, books and the television.

6. Think about new ways to express your love.

7. Say to your loved ones, "I love you because ..." and say something different each day until you run out of new things to say and then start over.

8. *Show* your affection with hugs and other physical contact. Break through any barriers that keep you from expressing your love by touching. Just do it and see how it feels and what the response is. Take the risk.

9. Bring home gifts when they are not expected. Follow your whims.

10. If you have trouble being open and spontaneous, play a little game with yourself. Pretend like you have been given the part of a carefree, loving, joyful, expressive person in a play. Put yourself into the part and go home and act it out. Do this often enough and the feedback you get will be so positive that the part will become natural and you will *be* that person.

When you have a loving relationship, *show it!* Be as affectionate as a puppy. Show your joy when a partner returns from a trip. If you don't feel joy, say so, and clear up all the feelings that get in your way of experiencing affection. Be free with smiles and gentle touches. Say reassuring words often and give compliments freely. If these things do not come to you naturally, practice them until they do.

When people break through inhibitions and express their love, the happiness game becomes a group sport with everyone supporting everyone else. I remember vividly an experience at one of the courses I attended. There was a conservative, macho type man there who rarely expressed his love to his family. He did not give many hugs. And he *never* hugged a man because that was a sign of weakness. In the process of our training, several men spontaneously expressed their affection for this man by giving him supportive hugs. The man in our group was amazed. He said he never felt love like that before.

When the course was over, the man's 26 year old son came to pick him up. And for the first time in years, the two of them hugged, said "I love you," and kissed each other. All of this was in front of hundreds of people. It as one of the most joyous moments of their lives, and those who witnessed the occasion also felt the joy that arises when two people are so openly loving and affectionate.

There is a bumper sticker that says, "Have you hugged your kid today?" Well, have you? Have you told your parents, your children, your friends, and your spouse "I love you" lately? If not, why not pick up the phone and do it now?

LOVE AND SEX

Love and sex are closely related. Nonetheless, there can be tremendous love with no sex and tremendous sex with no love. How can that be? You don't need a partner in order to have sex. You can have sex with yourself or with artificial contrivances. So sex and love can be separate.

But when they combine, the reaction is thrilling. Unfortunately, much of the literature today equates sex with orgasm. But they are not the same. An orgasm is a relatively short, very intense feeling. Sex based on love, on the other hand, is a lengthy, mutually stimulating interaction between two people. It does not necessarily lead to orgasm. In fact, orgasm usually ends sex.

Notice how we often ruin sex by concentrating on orgasm. Holding another person close is extremely nice. But is loses its beauty and wonder when it is compared to orgasm. For some people hugging is not enough, so petting becomes the next step. Again, great in and of itself, but usually not fully enjoyed because their mind is on orgasm. Finally, orgasm comes and enjoyment lasts for a short time and it is time to begin the ritual again. A person truly in the now could savor every moment of sex and not need climax, even though that may be the natural result.

Next time you make love, make love, not mutual climax. Enjoy every moment and keep in the now. Don't anticipate, don't rush, don't *think about it*. Experience your feelings fully. Be aware of your partner as well. Notice how he or she reacts. Stay in the now and notice how much pleasure one can get from sharing each other's feelings.

My wife and I learned about Marriage Encounter and found it helpful to our relationship. I've included an explanation of some of its concepts in Chapter 10. If you are interested, I urge you to study that section.

SCORING THE GAME

Clearly games are more fun when played with others. The game of life takes on a whole new meaning when we see others as part of an extended Self. Where does love fit into your life? How much love do you show Self and others? To see, score yourself from 1 to 10 depending on how accurately you feel the following statements describe you: 1 means the statement does not describe you at all, 10 means it describes you perfectly.

THE HAPPINESS GAME

DO YOU PLAY WITH LOVE?

Statement	Now	After 6 Months	After 1 Year
1. There is at least one person in the world who is as important in my mind as I am.	_____	_____	_____
2. I give myself under-standing, acceptance, patience, and genuine affection.	_____	_____	_____
3. I express my love for others openly, honestly, and spontaneously.	_____	_____	_____
4. I feel that the people closest to me are OK the way they are.	_____	_____	_____
5. I express my love with hugs and kisses and other physical signs.	_____	_____	_____
6. I do not *need* love from others to be happy.	_____	_____	_____
7. I do not rush love making, but enjoy it moment by moment.	_____	_____	_____

...continued

Playing the Game with Love

8. I regularly say "I love you" to those people in my life that I truly love.   _____   _____   _____

9. I realize that love of Self is the first step toward loving others.   _____   _____   _____

10. I like many people and many people like me.   _____   _____   _____

Total Scores   _____   _____   _____

Starting Date   _____   _____   _____

THE HAPPINESS GAME

Chapter 8

Playing With And For Others

*A*ll of the discussion in the book thus far has been mere preparation. Preparation for what? Getting control of *Self*. Maslow once called self-actualization the highest need of all. But he later found a need even greater than that: the need *to serve*.

Notice that I did not say "sacrifice Self for others" or "give up what you have for others," I said merely *to serve*. Let's say you have absorbed this book like a sponge and immediately put into practice all the concepts. You would be totally happy. But what then? There is only one joy beyond the joy of discovering *Self*; that is discovering *Others As Self*.

We have been talking as if *Self* were synonymous with you. At a certain stage of development, that is true. But beyond that stage is a whole new level of consciousness. That level is reached only by a few dedicated seekers. They are deeply involved in meditation (Zen) and other consciousness raising programs. What they discover is that there is no necessary separation between Self, environment, and others. Life depends upon a person having a heart, a liver, lungs, and a mind. They are all part of *Self*. But life also calls for food, air, water, and warmth. They are part of the environment, but they are as important to Self as mind or heart. Life depends on others. Others provide all kinds of life sustaining assistance. They defend us and feed us when we are too young to feed Self. In short, environment and others are all part of the whole *Self*. If we neglect their care, we neglect *Self*. When they get sick, *Self* gets weaker. When they flourish, *Self* flourishes.

The ultimate goal of the happiness game is to make Self complete. To do that means to serve all of Self, including environment and others. But this kind of serving does not take effort or a sense of loss any more than taking care of your *Self* takes any effort. The theme of this Chapter was expressed well by Hillel when he said, "If I am not for myself, who will be? But if I am only for myself, what am I?"

LETTING OTHERS BE

Many of the exercises in this book were designed to get control over your mind. The idea was to stop your mind from telling you that you were not capable or worthwhile. The ultimate goal was to accept yourself exactly as you are and as you are not.

The logical next step is to apply these techniques to learn to accept others exactly as they are and are not. That means not judging and criticizing them. It means *choosing* to have them be exactly as they are. It means choosing the world to be exactly as it is. You really have little choice, you know. Whether or not you choose the world as it is, it will stay as it is, at least for now. So why fight reality?

If you have gotten control over Self, you know how much better you feel as a result. When you get control over the universe, you will have an unbelievable feeling of contentment. The universe is your creation, after all. You are the one who *thinks* it is good or bad, supportive or nonsupportive. Your mind made those evaluations based on your beliefs. You can change them by conquering your beliefs, but your mind will fight you even harder on this one. It may let you accept yourself, but it has so much invested in its evaluation of others and the environment that it will resist change. It has thousands of prejudices, expectations, and conclusions it has developed over time. Your mind will defend these conclusions against any attempt to change them.

The game is this: If you can beat your belief system on this, you will gain a tremendous sense of happiness. Your environment and your fellow humans will be exactly as you would have them be. If your old beliefs win, you will always have a feeling of discontent. Your environment will always need changing and your fellow human beings will never live up to your expectations.

What a challenge! What a game! Is such a game too hard for you to play? Afraid you will lose? Well, not playing the game is certain failure — a forfeit. By playing the game and trying your best, you at least have a chance of getting closer to the goal. I choose you to play on my side. Let's go out and win: you win over your mind and I'll win over mine and we'll both accept each other as we are.

SERVING OTHERS

Once you choose yourself and everything else to be exactly as it is, you will have everything you always wanted. But it is not enough to have what you want; you must care for it or you will lose it. Just as you must care for your body, you must care for the rest of the world. It is your body and it is your world. You are responsible for them.

Notice that caring for the world should not seem like a burden any more than caring for Self should. It is part of life; it is necessary to sustain life. When a person suffers from hunger or pain or neglect anywhere in the world, you should feel the anguish. Others are all part of your universal Self. If you ignore them, they will ignore you, and you cannot live fully without them.

SELF ACCEPTANCE AND SERVING OTHERS

There is much criticism being expressed today about self help programs and books. Many people feel that such program encourage people to be selfish and to be totally "me" oriented. There is some truth in that. There have been a few books and programs with that orientation. But the vast majority of self-help books and programs are designed to develop people to their full potential, and no one can reach his or her full potential without serving others.

The first step in serving others is to self-actualize Self. Self must be educated, trained, matured, and molded into a self-sufficient, self-satisfied whole person. That person has much more to offer the world than a shy, introverted, untrained, and unsure person. A self-actualized person has much to offer: love, understanding, expertise, and objectivity.

Self development begins with self acceptance. Self acceptance provides a foundation for self development and improvement. Eventually Self will discover limits to growth. Those limits are imposed by environment and others. To maximize Self development means to fully develop the environment and others. Self, then, becomes synonymous with the universe. What is good for the universe is good for Self and vice versa.

Playing with and for Others

From that perspective, service to others and to the environment is not a burden; it is a natural consequence of a maturing *Self*. People reach out to others because others are as necessary to a full life as a body or mind.

You and I are responsible for the universe. If we want to play the game of life to its fullest, we must make the universe a good place to play. But you and I are mere grains of sand in the desert. How can we make a difference? We make a difference by caring, by joining together, and by trying. A few good people landed a vehicle on the moon, drove it around, and came back to earth. A few good people can make a similar impact on social development.

You have a critical role to play. You are required to play you. I will play me. Now let's go out and find others to play themselves. By letting them be themselves, we will find lots of friends. We can then bring those friends along to play the game.

We will start by making our communities better places to live. We can then influence our states and our nation.

A HAPPIER, MORE COOPERATIVE COMMUNITY

The community we live in often contributes or detracts from our quest for happiness. But a community is not an unchangeable entity. It is dynamic and ready to be shaped by its occupants. With the proper care, a community can offer comfort, and greater happiness to all its members.

The first step in developing a community that works is to establish a sense of community among the residents. There are many ways to get started including neighborhood picnics, block parties, and community association meetings. Once there is some feeling of community established, the next step is to determine community interests. Who is interested in a community garden, a food co-op, a jogging group, a book club? A community that works together not only gains a sense of belonging to a group, but a sense of well being and cooperation as well.

It is much cheaper to share with others in a community than to be an independent household. Sharing can begin with items such as fertilizer spreaders, lawn mowers, and snow blowers. Once a feeling of sharing and trust is established, such sharing can grow to include car pooling, meal sharing, shared baby sitting chores and cooperative house cleaning parties. The ultimate sharing experience is to trade skills, time, and nurturing behavior of all kinds. A plumber might fix a dentist's leaky faucet in trade for a dental check up. A mother who is not working outside the home can trade baby sitting time for appliance repair or medical care. Trading minimizes income taxes for everyone and contributes to a feeling of involvement that is worth much more than money.

An involved community can offer fire and crime protection as well. Each family is responsible for the others and volunteers can patrol the streets if necessary. Such cooperation leads to organizations such as "neighborhood parents." A child who must walk to school often may be several miles from home. It is comforting to see signs in windows throughout the community announcing that this is a home of a "neighborhood friend." The child can stop any time he or she gets caught in bad weather, is worried about strangers, or is lost. The neighbors keep in touch with each other by phone and create a safe environment for everyone.

Sharing and community protection are only the start of a happier, more supportive community. What really contributes to satisfaction is community work and play. Yes, I said *work* and *play*. It is fun to join community members in neighborhood clean-up, paint-up and fix-up parties. These parties often end with a neighborhood picnic or some similar activity. Work parties can add much to the physical surroundings. Neighborhood groups can plant trees and flowers. Recreation areas can be established and kept clean. And the neighborhood grows and prospers as one friendly unit.

Community pride can be fostered in apartment buildings, in townhouse developments, in suburban communities, in rural areas, and in the heart of the city. My wife and I were involved for six years in a townhouse community. We felt privileged to rear our son Joel in such a setting. We belonged to a food co-op, a baby sitting club, a play group and a tennis club. We joined in community picnics, earth days, craft shows, Easter egg hunts, and block parties.

People who moved from the community often wrote back saying they missed the community spirit and sense of belonging. What they need to do is establish similar groups in their own parts of the world. If everyone would practice community involvement, there would be giant steps made toward eliminating crime, improving schools, saving energy and generally creating a quality of life that makes for happier living for all. Marsha and I are thrilled to be in such a community now. We look forward to doing our part to make the community even better. We feel responsible; it is our community.

THE WORLD COMMUNITY

If we can share our tools and our talents with our neighbors, why not share them with the world? If food co-ops, clean-up groups, and safety patrols work locally, why not apply them on a larger scale?

Victory gardens were a popular nationwide effort during World War II. Could we feed all the hungry in the U.S. with a similar effort now? Could we feed all the hungry of the world with world-wide victory gardens? Who says it will not work — reality or mind? What is keeping us from trying?

With your help, I believe we can alleviate much of the hunger, disease, and suffering in the world. *Collectively we can make a difference.*

MAKING FRIENDS

If you and I are to succeed in our goal of making the world a better place to play the happiness game, we will need more friends to help. So let's talk about ways of making friends.

The secret for making friends is rather simple: To get a friend, be a friend. But what is a friend? A friend is someone who accepts you for what you are. So, to make friends, begin by accepting people as they are. A friend also is kind, supportive, helpful, and willing. To make friends, therefore, you should be all these things.

The most important trait of a person seeking friendship is being interested. People throughout the world seem more interested in one subject than any other — themselves. And they want others to be equally interested. To be their friend, therefore, you should show them that you like them, appreciate them, and understand them.

You express your interest in others by listening to them. Listen to what they say and listen to what they mean. To do that you must develop the ability to stay in the now when you are with others. You must focus full attention on them. No doubt you have noticed two things about most people: One, they do not seem to be listening while you talk. Instead, they seem to be looking for an opening to talk themselves. The second characteristic of many people is their tendency to let their eyes and minds wander as they carry on a conversation. They are obviously not "in the now," and do not seem at all interested in what you say. That is not the way to make friends.

To make friends, you must practice giving people your full attention. Show your interest in them by listening intently and asking questions. Your questions should give them a chance to express their ideas and show their special interests. If you make others feel important, you will win their friendship with little or no additional effort. You have given them the gift that surpasses almost all others, the gift of yourself and your time. When you make them feel good, they feel good about you. If you want others to speak well of you, speak well of them. If you want others to follow your leadership, follow their leadership and notice what games they enjoy.

LISTENING YOUR WAY TO FRIENDSHIP

There are several ways to improve listening skills which may greatly enhance our ability to make friends. The primary rule is the one we learned to counteract boredom: NO ONE AND NOTHING IS UNINTERESTING. Never *assume* anyone or anything is dull. People who are excited about subjects that *seem* boring should be given a chance to share their excitement with you. More often than not, their enthusiasm will become contagious and you will find yourself asking questions, trying to visualize what they're saying, and developing a new interest. At the same time, you may win a new friend, break away from old habits, and live life more fully. But all of this begins with the premise that you will try not to view anyone or anything as uninteresting.

And remember, like all things we treasure, friends need to be watched over and given our attention or we will lose them. I suppose Emerson says this best in just a few words: "We take care of our health; we lay up money; we make our roof tight, and our clothing sufficient; but who provides wisely that he shall not be wanting in the best property of all — friends?"

THE HAPPINESS GAME

FRIENDSHIP AND GIFT GIVING

There is no better way to maintain our friendships than to nurture them with the gift of our time and love. There are times when friends need us more than others, especially when they lose loved ones, when their careers lose their attraction, or when sickness strikes. At these times, close friends are there to listen and to support.

To some of us holidays are very sad occasions. Christmas, Passover and birthdays are particularly depressing because these are days we are supposed to be happy. But the tensions surrounding them often make them more of a chore than a joy. This can be especially true for holidays that involve gift giving. Who has not witnessed the crowds pushing and complaining during the holiday buying season? And for what? Could it be that we try too hard to enjoy ourselves and give of ourselves and end up not giving anything but gifts and frustrations?

What if we were to ban store-bought gifts for holidays? What would we give? The best gift of all — ourselves. For example, we could make something delicious to share with those we love. (Notice I didn't say cookies, cakes, and candy. Today's truly aware givers realize that such things are not good for others and give fruits and nuts and other nutritious gifts). We could give time or commitment.

On young lady in our community was separated from her husband and had three small children. Her friends wanted to give her something special for her birthday, so one offered five nights of baby sitting, another offered to cook five meals, and several others offered to help clean the house. Her friends gave of themselves. One day they all descended on her house to do spring housecleaning. They washed windows, mended, scrubbed, rubbed, and mowed. At the end of the day, they shared a meal and had a great time. How much more joy everyone got from this kind of giving rather than sending flowers or candy or buying another trinket.

Playing with and for Others

140

There is no reason for people to be sad during special occasions, but they must be made *special occasions,* not just another time to go shopping and give impersonal gifts. Some people have special talents they can share with others. Some people can sing or dance or play the piano, but how often do they share their gifts with friends? The best time to share talents, if not regularly, is during *special occasions.*

Everyone has some talent he or she can give others. Some people cook, others sew, still others read books. Some people have green thumbs, others are good mechanics, and still others are good painters. To put joy into special occasions, give gifts that it feels good to give. Give of yourself. Cooks cook, painters paint, and readers share their treasured books. No need to go shopping for such gifts. No need to worry about whether they will be appreciated. No crowds. No parking problems. No pushing. Only the joy of sharing with others, of giving *and* receiving friendship and love.

Holidays really become special when friends are so full of love that they seek others to share with. These people take some time on holidays to visit the sick or aged, spend some time with those in jail, or take an orphaned child home for dinner. Does gift-giving leave you cold? Are holidays periods of stress and strain? If so, isn't it time you stopped those traditions and start a new tradition of sharing your love and talents with those you love? You may want to spread your love to others in the community too. When you do, you will discover the happiness that comes from giving and you will know the real meaning of "special occasions."

Cultivating friendships is an art that takes much practice. Once you learn the art, you are ready to go into the world searching for new friends and new relationships. Once you master the art of drawing out everyone to find the interesting and the different, you can use that skill to discover new cultures and new horizons.

The person responsible for your full development is you. You are the source of your own happiness. The one person most responsible for making your world better is you. You are a key source of world happiness. "Why me?" you may ask. Who else? Who else is more qualified to serve others? All of us are in this game together. We all owe it to each other to play at our best and to help others play at their best. Where should we start? I'll begin by making my life better; you begin by making your life better. We start with *what is* and grow to *what can be*. From there we shall each tackle what comes next. We are likely to start with our families, our friends, and our community. We can then move to our state and our country. Then we can tackle our world. The happiness game has no boundaries.

SCORING THE GAME

The happiness game takes on a whole new meaning when we realize that the whole world is our playground. This feeling does not come easily, if it comes at all. But, it is interesting to follow our thoughts regarding brotherhood. How far are you able to reach out to others? Score yourself from 1 to 10 depending on how accurately you feel the following statements describe you — 1 means the statement does not describe you at all, 10 means it describes you perfectly.

DO YOU PLAY FOR HAPPINESS WITH OTHERS?

Statements	Now	After 6 Months	After 1 Year
1. I choose the world to be as it is.	_____	_____	_____
2. I feel my Self grow as I care for others.	_____	_____	_____
3. I live in or am working to create a caring and cooperative community.	_____	_____	_____
4. I feel I make a difference in the world.	_____	_____	_____
5. I have many friends.	_____	_____	_____
6. I am a good listener.	_____	_____	_____
7. I give gifts of time and understanding to my friends.	_____	_____	_____
8. I actively work to sustain my friendships.	_____	_____	_____
9. I participate in neighborhood, regional or national efforts toward improvement.	_____	_____	_____
10. I find everyone and everything interesting.	_____	_____	_____
Total Score	_____	_____	_____
Starting Date	_____		

THE HAPPINESS GAME

Chapter 9

Developing Strategies

*E*very once in a while, we learn a new way to approach a game that makes everything easier for us and helps us win. We could call any maneuver for gaining some advantage in life a happiness strategy. That is what this chapter is about — strategies for becoming a better player in the happiness game.

LEARN FROM OTHERS

No doubt you have heard the expression, "Experience is the best teacher." Actually, nothing could be further from the truth. Experience is an unthinking teacher that lets society make the same mistakes over and over. The truth is that, "Other people's experience is the best teacher." Any fool can learn from his or her own mistakes; the really intelligent person learns from the mistakes of others.

I've had students come into my office to tell me how awful Professor So and So is and how dull his course is. Since Professor S&S has been teaching at this school for years, students know that his class is dull, but every year they keep coming. Why? Because they never learn from the mistakes of others. To find the best professors and the most interesting classes, students need only ask other students ahead of them in the program. Sometimes a course is required and can't be avoided, but you can at least find the best professor to teach it.

Many students graduate from college and seek an interesting career. They often come back and tell me how miserable the training program is at Blank Corporation and how demeaning the work is. The students are learning through experience. Too bad. They could progress much faster in their careers and enjoy their jobs much more by learning from others who graduated a few years before them. Where are the interesting jobs? Which firms have good training programs? Where are salaries and working conditions best?

There are few things in life that haven't occurred before. Other people have faced the same problem you're having now. You can plod along learning on your own if you want, but the better way is to learn from others. If you want to learn to play tennis, read books written by the tennis teachers and take lessons from them personally. If you want to learn about happiness, study under the professionals.

This book is the compilation of my experiences searching for happiness. It was written so you could learn from my experience and pass it on to others.

AN INFORMATION SYSTEM

Major corporations throughout the world have developed an effective tactic to get more control over the huge amounts of information they deal with each day. They use what is called a management information system. The system monitors all environmental factors such as competitor prices, economic developments, and currency exchange rates. They also monitor internal information such as sales, profits, and employee turnover. All of us need to have a similar management information system to tackle the problem of making life work more joyously.

First let me illustrate the problem. People really enjoy taking vacations. Consequently, they read about vacation spots in newspapers and magazines and get some great ideas about where to go what to see, and what to do. Their ideas are very clear; but when vacation time comes, all that information becomes a little fuzzy. What hotel did that article recommend? Which tour was inexpensive, yet praised by all who went?

How can you keep track of information like that? Keep a file in your home with the title "Vacations." Every time you read something interesting about vacations, cut it out and put it in your file. At vacation time, all that information will be at your fingertips.

Now that you see the principle, notice how effectively it can be used to get more control over *all* of your interests. Do you enjoy new recipes but forget what it said in the paper? Set up a recipe file. My wife and I have files covering great places to eat, helpful household hints, gardening advice, and recommended consumer purchases.

The most important file of all is your happiness file. In it should be your list of foods you enjoy, places you enjoy visiting (including address, phone number, and brochures), things you enjoy doing (and not doing), and helpful hints for getting more fun out of vacations, work, and sports. If you hear about a good book to read,

THE HAPPINESS GAME

write it down and drop it in your file. Remember to periodically clean out these files so you'll have immediate access to the information you want.

My wife and I keep a calendar to plan our days to get in as many fun events as possible. We put in events such as our college's football schedule because we enjoy going to the games. We also write in parties, special community programs, and good TV shows. By keeping track of available opportunities, we seldom miss out on fun things.

A STRATEGY FOR SOLVING PROBLEMS

Don't think that a happy life is a life free from problems. There is no escape from problems except by dying. It is not problems that make life difficult, it is our attitude toward problems. Each problem should be approached as an opportunity to experience new success and explore new horizons.

On way to get rid of the myriad small problems that plague our everyday existence is to take on new, more challenging problems. I have a friend who is a doctor. I asked him if there were times when he felt discouraged, like when a patient suffered or an operation didn't go well. He said that those times occurred often. But he said he had a sure cure for ending those problems: he immediately tackled a new, more challenging case. By accepting a new challenge, he forgot about his past problems and never let life get him down.

So one strategy for solving problems is to accept a greater problem. The greater problem I have is to be more loving, more understanding, more open, and more giving to everyone I meet, including myself. Every day I wake with this problem facing me, and reaching for this goal has helped me forget dozens of little problems about myself. Life becomes better each day as I get a little closer to being the person I want to be.

Developing Strategies

STOP COPING AND EXPERIENCE

Dave was only 55 years old when his wife, Tina, died of cancer. Dave had no children and no relatives except a brother who lived thousands of miles away. He felt he had nothing when his wife died; nothing but his house and other "things." He contemplated suicide, but felt he could never see his wife in heaven if he did that. So Dave decided to learn to cope with his wife's death. He changed his retirement date to 65. Working helped him cope, and his friends supported him by offering him encouragement.

Five years later, Dave was still coping. His conversation was full of remembrances and regrets. His dead wife was his constant companion. Everything he did was done to cope with her death. But he seemed to be coping well and everyone admired how well he was getting along.

Dave might have lived his life forever in this state of semi-survival. But one day his friend George lost his wife in an accident. Dave went to George's house to help cheer him up and tell him how to cope. But George was grief stricken. He cried and cried and through his tears asked Dave if he had cried over the death of Tina. Dave *experienced* the loss of Tina for the first time as he and George discussed the tragedies that had come to them. Rather than cope any longer, Dave gave in to his feelings and joined George and cried until his eyes were red and swollen and then he cried some more. For more than a week, Dave experienced the anger, the disappointment, and all the other emotions triggered by his wife's death. And then it was over! He no longer had to cope. He quit his job and planned a retirement life full of new adventures. Dave's wife was now dead *and* gone. Coping had kept Dave from facing the reality of her death and had made him miserable. Letting all of his emotions out freed Dave to live his life on his own. Sure, he will miss Tina, but he will miss lots of things he had in his youth. There is a vast difference between feeling a loss and letting that loss dominate our thoughts and life.

THE HAPPINESS GAME

149

An effective tactic in the happiness game is to experience fully all that life offers. Experiencing the highs increases your enjoyment. But people try to avoid experiencing their lows. We try to cope with the loss of a loved one, with sickness and with divorce. But avoiding pain keeps it from going away. The more we try to cope, the more we think about it.

Try this tactic: *Experience* your pains and losses. Cry, talk about them, cry some more. Feel them deeply; really *experience* them. The terrible feeling will go away.

One day my wife and I visited a close friend in another state. We did not know it at the time, but he had just had a severe financial setback. He had lost his life savings in an investment and he was devastated. He could hardly force himself to look for a job but was embarrassed to talk about it and was doing his best to *cope.* I asked him if he had cried yet. Suddenly, he rushed from the house. He could not help but cry and he did not want us to see him. That is the answer to curing many of life's ills. Experience them fully, let all the emotions come out, cry, shout, and cry some more. Then the emotions will disappear and our naturally happy self will remain.

BRINGING GREAT MINDS HOME

The most stimulating of all experiences historically have involved the interplay of great minds. Many of these same experiences are available to you daily and are free of charge. They await you at your local library. Would you like to get to know Michelangelo and how he created the most marvelous statues in the world? Michelangelo's story is available in books such as *The Agony and the Ecstasy.* Great artists, politicians, and religious leaders, are willing to share their most intimate feelings with you. They await you at the library.

It's very said that many people never get beyond the movie magazines, and the sex stories. Even the newspapers are filled with stories that fill us with a sense of gloom. If murders, accidents, and political corruption are the only input your mind has, what can the output be?

Some people find books so alien to their experience that they cannot imagine themselves reading even the lightest of modern literature. Such people may find stimulation in television. It is unusual, I know, in this period of criticism to discuss TV as a source of inspiration. Yet there are dozens of programs such as the news shows, the talk shows, and the documentaries that bring to your home all sides of controversial issues presented by the best minds alive today.

I find it very expensive to subscribe to all the newspapers and magazines I enjoy reading. Instead, I take a couple of evenings a week and go to the library. There I can read for free. If I find articles I particularly want to keep, I copy them on the library's copier and put them in my file system. If I find a particularly good book or record, I simply check it out and take it home. I use the library often to find new books about happiness. One of those books showed me the benefits of visualizing as a happiness tactic.

LEARN TO VISUALIZE GOALS

Part of the excitement of a vacation trip is thinking about the fun we'll have. Those thoughts help us visualize not only the fun of vacations, but the fun of other projects as well.

For example, a neighbor recently began the difficult task of laying his own brick patio. The project called for carrying thousands of pounds of sand and bricks from the front of the house around to the back. It was a project that would take much of the spring. But he would often sit down with a group of friends and tell us all about the exciting parties and the fun he would have when the patio was finished. Whenever he would visualize the end at these meetings, he would rush home with new vigor to do more work on the project.

THE HAPPINESS GAME

151

One of the techniques managers use to motivate salespeople is to offer a vacation in Hawaii or another enticing place to the winner of a contest. Those salespeople who are able to visualize the pleasures of such a vacation find the selling task a means, rather than an end, and maintain a competitive spirit by keeping the goal in mind.

Visualizing, then, is a tactic that all of us can use to increase self-motivation. The time when visualizing was most effective for me was when I was debating getting my doctorate. I knew it would take three years and that the financial and personal sacrifice would be great. But I had the vision of being a university teacher who would inspire students and write interesting books. That inspiration supported me when things got tough. Visualizing is a dynamite tactic; use it often.

AN ENJOYMENT TACTIC

There is a great tactic for getting the most out of your experiences. When you are doing something new, stop for a minute and close your eyes. Pretend you are back home thinking about this experience. What would you have spent more time doing? What things would you have liked to see? Where would you have liked to go? Use these insights as guides for what to do next.

KEEPING SCORE OF AWARENESS

One of the best tactics for improving your game strategies is to keep track of what you are doing effectively and what you need to improve. How many first serves do you get in playing tennis? How many putts per golf green? How many minutes of jogging?

The same tactic is effective in keeping track of your progress in the happiness game. If you were to score one point for every smile or compliment or word of encouragement you gave to others and *Self* and took away one point for every frown, or disparaging remark, how many points would you have at the end of the day?

The idea is to increase your awareness. You might begin by scoring your relations with others. Don't cheat, for there is no winning or losing involved here. You know best what to put on the positive and negative side of your personal score card, but the sample on the next page might give you some ideas.

AWARENESS SCORE SHEET

Positive Actions (Score one point)

Saying a kind word
  to others

Staying in the now
  (5 points)

Enjoying serving others

Greeting others with
  a smile

Passing on something good
  you heard about another

Facing a stressful situation
  without getting upset

Being assertive about
  your rights

Giving your children a hug

Telling your spouse of your
  love

Praising the accomplishments
  of others

Telling the whole truth

Acting confident

Developing Strategies

Negative Actions (Substract one point)

Spreading rumors about others										
Greeting others with a frown or indifference										
Saying something negative about others — even in jest										
Being aggressive to win your rights										
Being passive to not offend anyone										
Criticizing anyone's efforts										
Telling lies or half truths										
Swearing										
Losing your temper										
Acting shy										
Categorizing Self or others										
Worrying about the past or wishing for something to change (minus 5 points)										

THE HAPPINESS GAME

DAILY GAME GOALS

Set game goals for each day: give yourself points for compliments, points for staying in the now throughout dinner, points for smiles and hugs and loving acts, and so on. At the end of the day, count up your points and set a new goal for tomorrow. Make it at least a (B) priority. Spend a few days just looking at positive points. Then spend a ew days recording negative points; negative points for any put downs of Self or others, negative points for stereotyping (*e.g.,* "I am dumb," "She is lazy," "All _____ are crazy.") and negative points for not being supportive.

In any sport, awareness is the key. If you *know* your elbow is bent when it should be straight, you can correct it. If you are not aware of your elbow, you are stuck. If you are aware of what increases your happiness and what interferes with it, you can improve. Without awareness you are stuck. Notice that you can use this tactic to improve any aspect of your life plan. This is what Ralph Waldo Emerson said about awareness of the now: "A man *is* what he thinks about all day long." What do you think about? Keep score and notice what your mind is doing. Then improve your game.

ASSERTIVENESS SKILLS

Another tactic for improving yourself is taking courses. One of the more popular courses over the last few years has been Assertiveness Training. Women and men who felt put upon, overly shy, or unaggressive, have taken courses to end that behavior. Assertiveness training is great for learning to get what is rightly and obviously yours. For example, you can learn to return an overcooked steak in a restaurant or to keep your place in line when people try to cut in. The problem is that some people mistake aggressiveness for assertiveness.

It is perfectly correct to say, "I was here first," to a clerk in a department store. This is being assertive. It is another thing altogether to burst to the front of the line and say, "I'm in a hurry, wait on me next." Assertiveness trainers have found it harder to teach aggressive people to tone down actions and be assertive than to teach shy people to speak out.

If you feel that people are taking advantage of you (remember, you cause those feelings), an assertiveness training course may be just what you need. Don't be afraid that such a course will make you bitchy or callous. Rather, it will help you see the difference between "helping others" versus "being taken advantage of," and taking responsibility for your feelings versus blaming others.

If you feel you would like to be more assertive, why don't you try these practice exercises?

1. Commit yourself 100% to being more self-assured and outspoken.

2. Note the times when you say "yes" to a request when you wanted to say "no."

3. Be honest with people when they ask you for assistance. Say "yes" only when you mean it.

4. Keep your agreements!

5. Practice being more assertive in your everyday contacts with others; state your views. Take the initiative and call up someone you would like to see and invite him or her over. Walk at the head of the group and sit in the front of the room. Walk erect and establish eye contact with people you meet. Be aware of your feelings and tell others if they do things that upset you (e.g., smoking, popping gum, etc.).

SCORING THE GAME

The goal of this chapter is to learn a few strategies for playing the happiness game better. Are you using these strategies? Score yourself from 1 to 10 — 1 means the statement does not describe you at all; a 10 means it describes you perfectly.

WHICH GAME STRATEGIES WOULD HELP YOU?

Statement	Now	After 6 Months	After 1 Year
1. I often seek the counsel of others before attempting a new task.	_____	_____	_____
2. I keep files of information I may use later.	_____	_____	_____
3. I solve problems by attacking the larger problem of being more open and more giving.	_____	_____	_____
4. I am not trying to cope with some bad experience from the past.	_____	_____	_____
5. I make optimum use of the library.	_____	_____	_____
6. I see everything I'd like to see on my vacations.	_____	_____	_____
7. I am assertive.	_____	_____	_____
8. I have a calendar where I schedule fun events.	_____	_____	_____
9. I set daily game goals for myself.	_____	_____	_____
Total Scores	_____	_____	_____
Starting Date	_____		

Developing Strategies

Chapter 10

Playing with the Pros

*B*ooks are an excellent tool for preparing you for new experiences and for reminding you of past experiences. This book does both. It has given you the foundation for creating your own happiness program. If you do the exercises and practice, you will win your own happiness game!

But some of you may want to practice the concepts of the happiness game in an environment where doubts can be aired, new techniques improved, and new friends made.

There are literally dozens of personal development courses

available. You should seek the one most appropriate for you, whether it be a shyness clinic, assertiveness training, a weight watchers program, or one of the more popular self-help programs. Below I shall review several of the most popular programs. My experience with them may not be your experience; I'm simply sharing what I have learned to give you a good foundation for seeking growth on your own. I do not necessarily recommend the programs discussed here above others. Nor do I feel you need to take any programs to be happy. All you need for happiness is a 100% commitment to do all the exercises in this book until your scores are *as high as you would like them to be!* Given that understanding, let's review what I've learned.

MEDITATION COURSES

There are three interesting approaches to awareness through meditation. Some of them are centuries old and are accepted in most countries of the world. Nevertheless, they are all relatively new to the United States. Let's see what they have to offer.

Transcendental Meditation

The founder of TM is Maharishi Mahesh Yogi. Because of his Eastern background, many people associate TM with some kind of religious philosophy, but it is not associated with religion at all. It is a technique that can be learned. You do not have to believe it will work or accept any philosophical ideas. You only have to learn the technique and the benefits will become apparent to you.

TM is taught in colleges and universities throughout the country. Its effects have been studied in some of the finest research laboratories in the world, including ones at Stanford, Harvard, and the University of Texas. Their findings have been published in Journals such as *Scientific American, American Journal of Physiology,* and *Science.* TM is not a fly-by-night, untested technique.

Transcendental Meditation or the Science of Creative Intelligence is taught in a course. The course consists of seven steps. At the first two introductory lectures the student is taught the basic elements of the technique and is given his or her own mantra. A mantra is a word or sound that is chosen especially for each student. That sound or word is what the student concentrates on in the process of meditating. These introductory classes are followed by an interview with the instructor. After that are four 1½ hour sessions of personal instructions over four consecutive days. During these sessions, the content varies based on the experiences of the student during meditation. The meditation experience has profound physical and mental effects on the body, so every care is taken to see that the process is done correctly. Things like going too quickly from meditation to work may cause headaches and other problems. Therefore, it is usually best not to practice TM without a course.

The basics of TM are rather simple. You merely meditate twice a day for 20 minutes each session. The mantra quiets all the babble in the brain. Thoughts come and go, but the meditator keeps coming back to the mantra.

The effects are similar to, but more powerful than, a long nap. Physiological tests of meditating people have found that oxygen consumption decreases rapidly — a sign of relaxation. Galvanic Skin Response (GSR) rates are high. GSR is a measure of nervousness; the higher the number, the more relaxed the person. In short TM allows people to relax mind and body. That results in greater perception, more energy, less tenseness, and a general feeling of happiness.

Biofeedback

Biofeedback is related to Transcendental Meditation in many ways. It is an attempt to make meditation more scientific. The idea is to monitor some function of the body by giving you feedback in the form of a sound or flashing light. Given this feedback, people are able to control bodily processes including heart beat and breathing. Using these processes, many people can lower their blood pressure, get rid of migrane headaches, and generally learn to relax.

The most interesting biofeedback machine monitors brain waves. It tells us how effective we are in shutting off conscious mind (beta thinking) to reach a different level of consciousness (alpha thinking).

Biofeedback is in its infancy compared to most meditation processes. It does have much promise. For now, I think you would enjoy trying the biofeedback machine to see how easily you can generate alpha waves. Any such device will help you become more aware of your various levels of consciousness. That is helpful in discovering Self.

Zen

Zen in Japanese means meditation. But Zen goes much deeper and further into it than transcendental meditation. Zen concentration is the kind demanded by race car drivers and other professionals whose lives depend upon total concentration. Unlike TM, though, this concentration is not closing off of the outside: it is a total awareness of what is happening. The conscious mind is focused, and the person remains alert, relaxed, ready. It is the mind set adopted by the participants in judo, kung fu and the other martial arts.

The process of learning Zen may take years rather than days. A Zen master will work with the student for days trying to alter normal mind patterns. One tool for such exercises is called a koan. A koan is a question that is impossible to answer — at least impossible using the kind of thinking we now use.

A key word in Zen might be attention. One simple Zen practice is to eat when you are hungry and drink when you are thirsty. Do you do that? Or do you eat breakfast, lunch, and dinner at some prescribed time?

Zen is beyond the coverage of this book. It is to meditation like a piano recital is to playing scales.

COMPREHENSIVE TRAINING

There is much skepticism associated with personal development programs, so I experienced them myself to give you my impressions. Here is what I found out about Marriage Encounter, est, Lifespring, Gestalt, Cornucopia, Encounter and Insight.

Marriage Encounter

Marriage Encounter is a short, intense educational program designed to increase communication skills between two people. Encounter is not for failing marriages; it is for good marriages that could be better or better marriages that could be all they can be.

The focus of Marriage Encounter is on Self as a unity of two individuals. We know that development of a relationship begins with two basically happy, secure people. Encounter builds self-confidence and self-sufficiency, but that is not the goal. That is only a first step in building a relationship.

Marriage Encounter is a spiritual process. It was developed within the Catholic Church, and is now sponsored by Protestant and Jewish groups as well. The role of religion in Marriage Encounter is to show couples the relationship between families and God and the world — period! It is not "church."

Marriage Encounter starts on Friday night and goes through Sunday. It begins with a presentation by a married couple who have completed the course. The presenters are not experts or counselors or therapists. They are simply two people willing to share themselves and their experiences with others. They go through the entire process *with* the 20-25 other couples taking the training. They are there to provide an example to show other couples that everyone is human and has difficulty communicating. They do not *prescribe;* they *describe* what is happening to them.

Marriage Encounter is about feelings. The only two people who count in an encounter are the two taking the course together. They make it work by their commitment to each other. They reveal, often for the first time, their true feelings about each other. They learn to stop judging, criticizing and begin communicating and loving. It is not easy at first. Each partner must go into a room and write a love letter to the other. The letter is designed to express feelings. Later the two get together in a room, exchange letters, read them twice ("once for the head; once for the heart") and then discuss them. This is just one of many opportunities to express in writing feelings about each other, love, sex, and other critical subjects.

It is important for communication to be written. Couples learn a pattern for talking with one another that often becomes a game and one player usually dominates the game. Both are trying to *win.* But written correspondence can be read and re-read carefully. Words can be written with great thought and without fear of interruption. Written communication is great for revealing true feelings.

Furthermore, an encounter weekend gives couples over 40 hours to communicate with *no other interruptions* — no children, no work, no football games on TV, and no obligations around the house. Much of the communication is nonverbal. Couples can sit and touch one another. They can look into each other's eyes and touch with their minds. Few couples communicate like that at home.

A Marriage Encounter weekend helps couples become *aware* of each other. It is a deeply moving experience. It can be more moving than many self development courses because it is *shared experience.* Two people learn to be happy as individuals and as a unity. Two people find that love is more powerful than any other feeling. Marriage Encounter does not end with one weekend. Couples are taught to write each other *every day.* No day goes by without time spent expressing feelings and love. The couple is supposed to follow a model called WEDS. It stands for *write, exchange, dialogue,* and *select.* It means that a couple should *write* for a *minimum* of 10 minutes their *feelings* about a particular topic. They are then to *exchange* their papers with each other. After reading these papers, the couple *discusses* what was said for a maximum of 10 minutes. Then a new topic is *selected* for the next day.

One of the exciting things about Marriage Encounter is that it prepares couples to make a difference in the world. Couples who love and respect each other cannot help but be more loving and respectful of others. Thus the process of love begins with self, grows into relationships, and spreads to the world and to God and the universe.

Est

One of the largest life education programs in the U.S. today is est. It stands for Erhard Seminars Training and consists of two intense weekends of discussion, exercises, and life experiences. Est is comprehensive in that it is based upon many of the other programs that are designed to make life work: Zen, Gestalt, Encounter, Yoga, and others. Werner Erhard carefully studied all of these programs in his own personal search for meaning in life. One day he experienced a transformation; he suddenly saw for the first time what all those programs were about. No one can describe what transformation is; we can only experience it ourselves, so Werner started est to create the environment in which others can transform their lives.

Est and many of the other programs are very helpful because they put the responsibility for changing a person's life where it belongs — on that person. Often people wonder how est can change lifelong patterns in only 60 hours or so. Think of it this way. The average college course consists of 30 hours in the classroom. In such a course, one can learn all the fundamentals of subjects such as biology, calculus, Latin, and more. Since est is 60 hours, it is the equivalent of *two* college courses — quite a bit of knowledge about the game of life.

Most people know a little about est, and in this case a little knowledge is a dangerous thing. So much of what happens in the training *seems* peculiar. People often have questions about the rules covering bathroom breaks, questions about the language used by the instructors, and questions about the pressures some participants feel.

One reason est seems so full of questionable practices is because the training simulates lives. Life is full of people who swear, people who keep us from doing what we want, people who question our beliefs, people who yell, and people who are mean. And, one problem with life is that we rarely learn how to deal with those people. Est teaches us how to cope and est also teaches self confidence. But est does more than give one control. It helps give shy people confidence. It enables compulsive talkers to listen better. It helps people conquer fears and shows the fearless how to open to others sometimes means giving up the "hero game." Est helps people control anger and allows people to be angry. It shows what true love is and how to better relationships. It is much of the training from other self-development programs combined into one.

Does it work? Yes, when people let it work. Does it last? Yes, because what changes is the trainee's perspective on life. People are transformed and that transformation continues through life. Does it solve all of life's problems? No, but it gives direction to those trying to tackle their problems. When I took it, est cost $350. A few graduates feel the cost is too high, but you have to decide what the value of a controlled life is to you.

I cannot tell you any more about est because I have promised not to, but I can tell you this. During the first weekend, I learned about getting rid of those beliefs and those behaviors that made me less of a person. I learned to break through my games and to be more loving. I learned to begin accepting people as they are and how to improve my relationships.

The second weekend I learned about the games I play and how they hurt my ability to play the happiness game. I also learned to be more aware of my senses and emotions. I learned about love, sex, and relationships. At the end, I learned about me.

A Note About Graduates

A human potential movement graduate is much like a reformed alcoholic or cigarette smoker. They often feel they have found the TRUTH and are eager to share it with you. As a consequence, they will often come on too strong. They sometimes forget that you may not be one of *them*. You are living in the "real" world. You do not "believe" yet.

Try to understand. They love you in a way you may not comprehend. They want very much to be open and honest and expressive with you. They want to give you the freedom to do likewise. Can you blame them for wanting to share that with others? Of course they are awkward at it, it is new to them. They have been playing a different role for years and this one is very different to master in a world of unresponsive people. They will settle down eventually and live a quieter life. And they will live it happier. Like an overprotective parent, they will try to get you to experience est too.

Talk to your friends who have graduated from self development programs. Notice their enthusiasm. They are being honest. They want you to experience life as fully as you can and to let them do the same. They want to be more honest, more open, and more expressive, and more loving. They are happier with themselves and are eager, oh so very eager, to share themselves with others. Give them a chance. Maybe you too will join the human potential movement. Personally, I want you to be free to become all you can be. If all the people in the world felt free to be themselves and to live their lives openly and honestly, they would let you and me do the same.

I am one of those graduates who got great value out of personal development courses, but you should approach such courses with some caution to be sure you are doing what is best for you. Talk to your friends who have gone or seek out people with some experience. Talk to a counselor. Personally, I talked with many people before I took any course. My wife is one of several who supports Lifespring. I enjoyed it myself, but recent criticisms in the media show that careful research is needed before recommending that others go. Let's review my experience.

Lifespring

I took Lifespring a couple of years after I took est. I found many of the concepts to be the same, but I also learned some new concepts and techniques for playing the happiness game. Both est and Lifespring start off slowly. You are likely to feel uncomfortable at first. As the training progresses, you may experience the full gamut of emotions from anger to love and from boredom to elation. Lifespring teaches people to be honest, loving, and expressive. People who have never said "I love you" to their parents or children, often do so after the training. They have learned to be more open about their feelings. They are more truthful about how they feel and they show their feelings by their actions (e.g., hugging, smiling, sharing, and being there when needed).

It is not easy to be open with people, and many trainees in Lifespring have to confront those fears. But they learn to break through the walls that separate them from others and to shed their inhibitions. In short, they learn to "go for it" when they want something in life. And the results are unbelievable!

As with est, I would not hesitate to recommend the basic Lifespring training to my family or my friends. I know it would enrich their lives tremendously to learn the principles of self-enrichment and reaching out to others. But there are differences between est and Lifespring that are rather significant. In Lifespring, the participants interact with one another one-on-one and in small groups. This enables people to practice new behavior patterns and to express their feelings more openly. Est encourages sharing, but not on a one-to-one basis and not as often. The basic Lifespring training is often described as more "gentle," and more "supportive" than est. In fact, both groups are very supportive. Est simply forces people to confront their beliefs more intensely. By the last day, though, most est and Lifespring graduates are transformed people who are better able to handle themselves, others, and the world. Lifespring costs $350.

Lifespring graduates are often so enthusiastic that people are skeptical about the results. "How can so many people get so much in so short a time?" they ask. Lifespring has anticipated such skepticism. Unlike most other self improvement programs, Lifespring is guaranteed! If you don't get value out of the training, your money is quickly refunded. In fact, you sign a money-back guarantee before you start. I found that incredible. But the training is so helpful that few ask for their money back.

You will learn how to get more control over your mind so that you can live more in the now. But does it last? The answer, I feel, is yes. The training teaches you new perspectives, new attitudes, and new confidence.

Graduates of Lifespring generally feel ready to play the happiness game with enthusiasm. Most of them have made a commitment to be 100% involved in life and to live up to their agreements. They know better what they want and what limiting beliefs have been getting in their way.

Insight

Insight is very similar to Lifespring. Many of the processes are similar, as are the results. Insight may be even more loving and supportive. My group was, but it may have been the size (I was in a smaller group of 100), or the dynamics of those particular people. I doubt it, though.

Insight was very special for me. The results are the same as those I have described for Lifespring. (The basic training now costs $275.)

If you have never experienced opening your heart to a large group of people and making yourself totally vulnerable to them, you cannot understand the warmth, affection, and love that is possible in such a setting. I don't understand it either. I only know what it feels like, and it is wonderful. Insight is not a religious group, yet the spiritual feeling of love draws many participants closer to God. When one learns to love Self and others, one is further along the path to God, whatever that path may be.

If all this talk about love and acceptance leaves you skeptical, I know what you mean. I was too. But one thing that makes life work is to break through skepticism and try things that may make life more beautiful. Insight is one of those things.

Cornucopia Institute

One of my favorite self-help books is *Handbook to Higher Consciousness* by Ken Keyes, Jr. I encourage you to read this book, for it is the basis for another helpful organization. It is called Cornucopia, a center for human awareness located on 150 acres in Kentucky. It is a community of Residents "dedicated to creating a world where love is allowed to flow freely from human heart to human heart." The center offers one-week, one-month, and three-month trainings. It also offers workshops in the "Living Love Way" in many major cities in the United States. If you read the book by Ken Keyes, you will see what it is all about. Here again you will learn how to be more accepting of yourself, more open to others, and better able to handle life's challenges.

Cornucopia also offers courses such as "Opening Up" where participants are able to look at the suffering they create — anger, jealousy, guilt — and free themselves from these and other emotions that separate them from others. Courses called "Getting Free-er,"

"Loving Relationships," "Joy of Living," "It's OK To Be Me," "Touch the Earth," "Special Stuff," and "The Road to Happiness" give some indication of what is available. At this time courses range in price from $75 to $650.

ENCOUNTER GROUPS

Maybe you want to try one of the older, more established groups that provided the foundation of these newer groups. Let's look at Gestalt Therapy, for example, and see what it offers.

Gestalt Therapy

The driving force behind Gestalt Therapy is Frederick (Fritz) Perls. He did not accept the popular therapies of Freud because he felt they tried to "help" people when "help" is the last thing they wanted. According to Gestalt Concepts, the path to growth and the development of human potential is *awareness*. Gestalt therapy consists of specific strategies and techniques that lead toward greater *awareness* and *self reliance*. The basic concept behind Gestalt is that maturation is a continuous growth process in which environmental support is transformed into self-support. People in Gestalt are not "helped;" they are guided to take personal responsibility for maturing.

The "voice" we talked about earlier (the one in your head) is what Perls calls Topdog. Topdog is that inner voice (and sometimes some outer voice of "authority") that keeps a constant flow of words running through your thought system. Topdog is demanding, critical, and moralistic. It almost constantly asks questions like "Why did you do that?" or "Why are you so clumsy?" It gives orders to "Be careful," "Try harder" and "Wake up, dummy."

According to Gestalt, Topdog has someone inside you who listens. The listener's name is Underdog. Underdog is highly skilled at pretending to listen to Topdog while really goofing off. Underdog says, "But I'm trying so hard, I'll do better next time," or "I'll do it as

THE HAPPINESS GAME
171

soon as I can," or "What can you expect, I'm not good at this." Underdog *seems* like the weaker of the two tyrants, but it usually wins. Of course, that causes Topdog to say all kinds of mean, cutting remarks, which Underdog reacts to by being even more incompetent.

Gestalt Therapy is one technique for stopping that constant dialogue going on in the mind. People have two sources of personal support in the game of life: one is the *now* with its experiences, emotions, and realities. We always seem to have the resources to handle now in our life; it is the tomorrows and the yesterdays that cause so much pain. The other source of support is the fantasy world of wishes, dreams and beliefs. Gestalt Therapy is based on the fact that the only reality in life is the *now,* the *here,* and the Self.

The problem with people, according to Gestalt Therapy, is that they get stuck in some uncompleted situation from the past. Perls calls it an "impasse." People would rather maintain the assured status quo of a failing marriage, a mediocre aliveness, or a lousy self image than to cut through to the unknown world of responsibility. Often people keep stuck in the impasse because it gives them someone else to blame for their problems. Often that person is a parent or a spouse. "I'm like I am because my mother hated me" becomes an excuse for a life that permits all kinds of faulty behavior.

Gestalt Therapy uses dreams as a vehicle for "unsticking" people. According to Gestalt the objects and persons in our dreams are really separate parts of our own personality. By focusing on these separate elements, Gestalt tries to create a whole person (gestalt) who is so centered that Topdog and Underdog and fantasies and personal history are all dissolved in the realization of *now.* To break through the impasse, Gestalt has a person act out various dream roles. At no time does the person receive any "help." The idea is to face the conflicts of the past and resolve them in a one-person dialogue between dream components.

The purpose of all of this is to increase awareness. But a person cannot achieve awareness until all "unfinished business" is cleared up. Unfinished business includes unresolved parent/child conflicts, continuing sibling rivalries, and much more. Dream dialogues help discover what the "unfinished business" is and *finishes it.* That leaves the person open to awareness of the now.

Gestalt is one form of what are known as encounter groups. The major difference is that in Gestalt the group leader interacts on a one-to-one basis with participants in some kind of rotation. In most encounter groups, the interaction is among participants.

Gestalt Therapy is very evident in est and Lifespring seminars. This is all very reassuring to someone trying to learn the happiness game. Most of the professional instructors of the game are playing from similar playbooks. Some use one technique, others use some other technique, but all are in general agreement about some basic points. I will close this section with the Gestalt Prayer:

I do my thing, and you do your thing.
I am not in this world to live up
     to your expectations,
And you are not in this world to live
     up to mine.
You are you, and I am I,
And if by chance, we find each other,
     it's beautiful.

THE HUMAN POTENTIAL MOVEMENT

The human potential movement reached its zenith sometime in the late 1960s. It was in this period that encounter groups were at their peak. The names of the groups include T-groups, Bion, process groups, Esalen, marathon groups, and others.

Let's review some of the basic concepts behind these groups. Then we can discuss some specifics about techniques. Basically, encounter is an educational, recreational, and spiritual process that is based on honesty, openness, and self-responsibility. It is educational in that participants learn about themselves and how they relate to others. It is recreational in that participants are free to express themselves in song, dance, and expression so that the process can be quite fun. The process is spiritual in that there usually is an emphasis on the idea that "God is within" or that God works through you.

A key word in encounter groups is "energy." People use up energy by being emotionally tense, defensive, and protective of their beliefs. Body awareness techniques reveal signs of uptightness such as shortness of breath, stomach pains and chest pains. Awareness leads to a desire to change, and encounter offers needed help.

I suppose that the major benefit of encounter groups is enhanced awareness of social interaction. Participants are encouraged to express themselves with nonverbal as well as verbal communication. For this reason, people tend to associate encounter groups with the touchy-feely school of self-help. In fact, there is usually much body contact in encounter groups, but such contact can be overemphasized by outside observers. The whole idea is to learn to relate to others. Sometimes that calls for expressions of love, and that leads to hugging, hand holding, and other signs of support.

Encounter groups differ from traditional psychoanalytical therapies in that encounter does not care about what causes neuroses; it only wants people to do something about them. The process starts when a group of people (8-15 or more) get together in some relaxed setting. At first there is little structure so that people can *experience* the normal tension that occurs in group settings. Eventually the group forms some kind of structure and discussion begins. Participants are encouraged to give "feedback" to other participants that reveal how people are perceived by others. Participants will point out, for example, body movements, facial expressions, voice patterns, and behavioral patterns. All of this feedback makes people more aware of what they do and how it affects others.

Eventually the group's discussion will focus on group behavior patterns. It will discuss role behavior and the games people play. Some participants will be aggressive and irritable. Others will be shy and passive. Some will hide their feelings behind a smile; others will hide themselves behind words or gestures, or by withdrawal from the group. As each person becomes more aware of the games he is playing (self-discovery), the process of social development can begin (self-responsibility and self-fulfillment).

Techniques for self-expression include psychodrama, case studies, and discussion sessions. Psychodrama is a very old technique that is basically play acting. For example, a quiet person may be asked to play the role of an outgoing party-goer. People who have unresolved conflicts from the past (a Gestalt concept) may be asked to play all the roles of the people involved. People who are very self conscious may be asked to dance or sing or give a speech. People are encouraged to do what they are most reluctant to do. Thus participants have a chance to try new ways of relating to others, new ways of self expression, and new ways of behaving, in a "safe" environment. People accept each other as they are first and then assist them to become all they can be.

What people learn in encounter groups is *responsibility*. The greatest responsibility, of course, is to be yourself and be all you can be. No one in encounter groups will be there to hold a person's hand after he graduates. Rather, a graduate learns to rely on *Self*.

THE HAPPINESS GAME

TRAINING COURSES:

Below are the addresses and some basic information about the training courses I have mentioned. Which one is best for you depends on where you are in life, what problems are bothering you, and what your goals are. Listen to your friends who are graduates. They know you better than anybody and can share their experiences from the trainings. The following list will help if you write for more information:

est
765 California Street
San Francisco, California 94108
Basic Training: $350
Available in more than 27 cities in U.S. and in India,
   England and Canada.

Central Lifespring Office
4340 Redwood Highway/Suite 50
San Rafael, California 94903
Basic Training: $350. Graduate Training: $750.
Available in 9 cities in the U.S. and in Canada.

Cornucopia Institute
St. Mary
Kentucky 40063
Courses range in price from $75 to $650
Write for details

Gestalt Directory
P.O. Box 275
Highland, New York 12528

Insight Training Seminars
1619 Wilshire Boulevard
Santa Monica, California 90403

Basic training: $275, Graduate Training: $975
Available in Philadelphia, Washington, D.C.,
   Los Angeles and other cities. (It's new so write for
   other sites.)

SCORING THE GAME

No one *needs* to take a course in personal development because no one is "good" or "bad" as they are. We are all at different stages of development in becoming happy, loving, active, involved people. No one needs to study anything. On the other hand, it is great fun to learn to play music and to play all kinds of sports. It is even more fun, in my opinion, to learn to play the happiness game. Let's take another look at your progress in the happiness game. I hope you will keep playing for life. Score yourself from 1 to 10 depending on how accurately you feel the following statement describes you. 1 means the statement does not describe you at all; a 10 means it describes you perfectly.

WHAT PROGRESS HAVE YOU MADE?

Statement	Now	After 6 Months	After 1 Year
1. Overall, I am a contented, satisfied, happy person.	————	————	————
2. I fully enjoy every day and everything I do.	————	————	————
3. I know I have enough in life now.	————	————	————
4. I find it easy to love others and to make friends.	————	————	————
5. I know I do not *need* to take personal development courses, but I am open to learning about myself.	————	————	————
6. I love my Self and Others.	————	————	————
7. I am enthusiastic about life.	————	————	————
8. I was able to read this book and explore my life without judging myself or comparing myself to others.	————	————	————
9. I am me, and that is great.	————	————	————
10. I am happy now.	————	————	————
Total Scores	————	————	————
Starting Date	———————————————————————		

Playing with the Pros

CONCLUSION

This last exercise is not meant to be the end of your search for happiness. Rather, it should be merely the beginning. Try putting the book aside for a few months and then read it again. Write down concepts you particularly like. Do the exercises and watch your progress.

Meanwhile, try being more aware of your Self, your environment and other people. Notice also how difficult it is to change any of your beliefs. Most of us seem stuck with the way we are. We do not necessarily like it, but we tend to feel that we are what we are and that is that. It is true that we are what we are, but that is far from the end of it. Tomorrow is a whole new day. It is, as they say, the first day of the rest of our lives. It can be the first day we are truly happy and alive and loving.

But most of us need help, and that is where the human potential movement comes in. You can pick from dozens of interesting and challenging educational programs designed to assist you in assisting yourself. They are as important to a basic education as English, history, math, and reading. Sign up for one of the personal growth programs in your area. Go after happiness with determination and zeal. Have a good game.

Index

Index

182

THE HAPPINESS GAME